To Fly through the Air

TO *Fly*

THROUGH THE *Air*

The Experience of Learning to Fly

Tom Morrison

Iowa State University Press / Ames

Tom Morrison is a professional mining engineer and a dedicated private pilot. Born and raised in England, he gained his first experience as an underground miner in England, West Germany, and Canada. After graduating from the Camborne School of Mines, he emigrated to Canada in 1976. Since then he has followed an adventurous career in mining and tunneling all over North America. Since 1982 he has made his home in British Columbia, working in mining, mineral exploration, and heavy construction. He is the author of three books on British mining history and of numerous technical and historical articles on mining and tunneling. He is also becoming known as an aviation writer.

©1991 Iowa State University Press, Ames, Iowa 50010
All rights reserved

Authorization to photocopy items for internal or personal use, or the internal or personal use of specific clients, is granted by Iowa State University Press, provided that the base fee of $.10 per copy is paid directly to the Copyright Clearance Center, 27 Congress Street, Salem, MA 01970. For those organizations that have been granted a photocopy license by CCC, a separate system of payments has been arranged. The fee code for users of the Transactional Reporting Service is 0-8138-0348-9/91 $.10.

⊗ Printed on acid-free paper in the United States of America

First edition, 1991

Library of Congress Cataloging-in-Publication Data

Morrison, Tom (Thomas A.)
    To fly through the air: the experience of learning to fly / Tom Morrison. — 1st ed.
        p.   cm.
    ISBN 0-8138-0348-9
    1. Flight training. I. Title
TL712.M67 1991
629.132'52—dc20   91-8191

Contents

Preface,   **VII**
Acknowledgments,   **XI**

1. Cleared for Takeoff,   **3**
2. The Dream,   **6**
3. Why?   **17**
4. Discovery Ride,   **21**
5. Sprog,   **26**
6. Circuits and Thuds,   **35**
7. Solo,   **41**
8. Back to School,   **46**
9. Around the Patch,   **49**
10. Over the Hills and Far Away,   **56**
11. Up Island,   **63**
12. Going for a Spin,   **68**
13. Judgment Day,   **72**
14. On the Gauges,   **77**
15. The Dark Sky,   **83**
16. Things that Go Bump in the Night,   **90**
17. Through the Clouds,   **94**
18. Interlude: Gone Flying,   **100**
19. That First Hundred Hours,   **104**
20. The Commercial Ticket,   **109**
21. Style,   **114**
22. Black Boxes and White Magic,   **119**
23. Needles in a Dark Haystack,   **127**

24. Further and Better Particulars,   134
25. Blowing in the Wind,   140
26. A Spreading of Wings,   146
27. Precision,   152
28. VFR, a Very Frustrating Restriction,   158
29. Aerobic Exercises,   165
30. Cloud Nine,   172
31. The Last Battle,   179
32. Cleared for the Approach,   186

Preface

What is it like learning to fly? You must be wondering, or you probably would not be looking at this book. You can find books, of which there are many, with the generic title *How To Fly an Airplane*. Even if you read such a book from cover to cover, at the end you will not be able to fly an airplane. Nor will you have answered your question. You will be left wondering what it is *really* like. Is it a deep spiritual experience or a series of mechanical manipulations? Or neither? Or both? Or sometimes one, sometimes the other? Is "to fly an airplane" the same as "to fly," and, if not, which do you learn by taking flying lessons? They cost enough, so it would be nice to know.

There is an ever-present, ever-changing dichotomy between operating an aircraft and flying. If a Cessna 172N single-engined landplane is accelerated from rest on a hard, level surface until its indicated airspeed is 73 knots, and if the aircraft is then rotated in the pitching plane by +6°, the angle of attack, and hence the lift coefficient of the wing, will be increased to a value such that the lift force exceeds the gross weight of the aircraft and it will leave the ground. That is to say, in common parlance, it will fly. Furthermore, the pilot receives sensory inputs, which his brain has acquired the capability to analyze, which indicate to him that the aircraft's aerodynamic parameters have reached, or are reaching, values which will permit free flight. How dull! Let's try that again.

There comes a point in the takeoff roll when your being expands all through the aircraft, out to the wingtips, through the engine into the propeller blades, out to the tip of the tail. Merging with the wind, you feel the lift force growing all through you. You have become a flying creature, launched from its lair, armed only with knowledge and cunning, to prowl the unforgiving ocean of the sky. You have just done what has eluded all but four of the past generations of mankind. You in your solitude have affirmed your unity with a great stream of human endeavor, the furthest ramifications of which reach out into the ultimate enigma of space. Flight is a many-faceted thing; the learning of it is strange.

You must be curious about flying; otherwise this book would not be in your hand. Perhaps a flight in a light plane or the experiences of a friend have sparked your curiosity. Perhaps you saw a small airplane fly overhead and your spirit reached up toward it. Perhaps you want to be an airline pilot, or an Air Force pilot, or even a space pilot, or maybe you just want to fly. No one is born knowing how to fly, not even a bird. Everyone has to learn, and most people, with a negligible number of exceptions, start to learn in a little itty-bitty putt-putt airplane with a matchstick propeller whirling around its nose. Yet you realize that flight is a large adventure on which to embark, perhaps the biggest of your life. And you wonder what it is really like. Not least among the joys of flight is giving it to others. This book is my gift to you. If I have done my job well, it may tell you something of what the learning is like.

This is not a how-to-fly book; it is a what's-it-like book. This is what it is like learning to fly a light aircraft as a civilian in North America in the 1980s. There are plenty of books on flight, but only a few will describe the learning to you. There are sources of information which will give you numbers and tell you of hours and dollars, but not all the sources are unbiased, and between the flighted and the flightless is a gap in experience which this book will seek to bridge.

Two or three of us used to drive together to private pilot groundschool. We were all at the same stage, delving deep into our instructors' stores of patience, adding years of wear and tear to the unfortunate airplanes with the impact of our returns to the all too solid ground. We battled with powerful but inchoate fears which we were loath to admit. They gave us a thick book in small print, which read, in part: "No pilot shall, while operating under IFR, operate a transponder responding to Mode A/3 interrogation other than as directed by ATC." We trembled in unison without a clue what it meant.

We watched Real Pilots sauntering out to their aircraft. They would be airborne and leaving the neighborhood in the time it took us to reach item #3 on the pre-start checklist. They obviously had what it took to refrain, while operating under IFR, from operating a transponder responding to Mode A/3 interrogation other than as directed by ATC. They had the Right Stuff. We asked each other: "How on earth (or off it) do *we* get *there* from *here*?" This book will shed light on the process.

Acknowledgments

This book did not come into being in isolation. A number of people have participated, wittingly or unwittingly, in its conception, writing, and production.

A long succession of school teachers, university lecturers and tutors, magazine and book editors, and work colleagues all made their contribution over a span of some thirty years by demanding that I write proper English. They praised when praise was due and criticized ruthlessly when criticism was appropriate. For the most part they were English people of the old classical tradition and nothing, no woolly thought, no sloppy expression, no grammatical error or misplaced punctuation, escaped their piercing gaze. To them I owe a debt of gratitude for teaching me to express myself in written English.

My next thanks must go, of course, to the Victoria Flying Club at Victoria, British Columbia, not only to the instructors but also to the staff and directors who made sure that the organization continued to exist (no mean task at times!) and ran efficiently. Two flying instructors, Doug MacColl and Jack Kaiser, figure prominently in these pages and it should be clear that my regard for them is unbounded. The Flying Club also provided a stage on which a number of amusing little episodes were acted out and a venue through which lasting friendships arose among people who would never otherwise have met. We were all from the most diverse walks of life, but all linked by our common fascination with flight.

My thanks are due to the Iowa State University Press and especially to Mr. Bill Silag, Managing Editor, who saw the good in the original manuscript and told me to improve upon it, rather than either publishing it as it was or rejecting it out of hand. Bill, too, was the primary recipient of scathing rebuttals of readers' comments and querulous inquiries as to the progress of the book through the publication process. Thanks are also due to the production staff for their traditional adherence to high standards of workmanship.

Tom Morrison

Vancouver, British Columbia

To Fly through the Air

1

Cleared for Takeoff

"X-Ray Mike Yankee cleared for takeoff, runway one eight. Through fifteen hundred feet contact Vancouver Departure on one twenty point five."

"X-Ray Mike Yankee" is the radio callsign for a ton and a half of IFR-equipped Cessna 182 aircraft.* The rumbling and chuckling of the 230-horsepower engine swells to the roar of a furnace. The square-bladed propeller flails the air; the black asphalt flows beneath the aircraft; the lift force blossoms around the wings; the bird flies. At 300 feet above the ground, flaps up and power back to 23 inches of manifold pressure. The harsh bellowing of the engine eases to a smooth singing; the aircraft shifts its balance and settles into the sky for which it was made.

We sweep out toward the radio beacon in a maximum-performance climbing turn. This is an IFR departure, and soon we will forsake the familiar perspectives of the earth for that surreal other world of the clouds. Tiny puffs of mist slide past, but the main base of the overcast is still above, dappled gray. At 2,000 feet our climbing path is barred by a wall of amorphous vapor. We look at it. It waits. Suddenly we are inside it, still climbing. We level off in cloud at 4,000 feet.

As suddenly as passing through a door, we break out into a cloudscape of unearthly beauty. This is the high country of the sky, IFR territory, the sky of the instrument pilot. We are flying through vast halls, softly carpeted with dove-gray cloudlets, walled with slate-gray columns, roofed with soaring vaults and buttresses and gargoyles,

---

* Phonetics for the last three letters of the aircraft's Canadian registration letters C-GXMY. IFR stands for "instrument flight rules."

splashed with sunlight. My aircraft and I are running, laughing, bursting through mists, now lofted in the upwelling froth of clouds, now peering down into dim chasms, and we are happy.

There is joy in the sunlit heavens, but a tinge of sorrow for those who cannot share this with me and for all the past flightless generations of mankind. There is disciplined precision in this flight and in the immutable law of the sky, but at the same time there is utter freedom. There can be no freedom without responsibility. Up here in the wild sky, the responsibility is absolute; so is the freedom.

There is peace, which is the total victory, after bitter struggle, over mind-crushing fears of separation from the solid earth. The fear that strove to chain me to the ground is now my servant to warn me of danger. On occasion I will take counsel with it and not fly on a certain day, or by a certain route, or in some particular aircraft, but I have trodden it down and stamped on it, and it has no power over me.

There is deep gratitude for health of body and mind, for the gifts of perseverance and self-discipline, for this aircraft and this sky, and for everything that has gone into making this moment come true.

But why am I here? I am no professional pilot. I am a mining engineer, paid to make holes in the ground for other people. I am here because I wanted for twenty-three years to learn to fly. This flight is the culmination of three years of flight training and study and practice on evenings and weekends and on days pried loose from a busy routine to steal away and fly. Three years in which, by infinite toil and at great cost, I learned to spread my wings and fly.

My first lesson had been to discover how vast and all-encompassing was my ignorance and incapacity. I learned the apparently simple skill of holding the aircraft in straight and level flight, then to turn, to climb, to descend, to take off, and, after months of frustrated bewilderment, to accomplish the mystery of returning to earth. I flew solo: I flew to far-off places. I fought the subtle terror that lurked in the solo spin, and won.

Then a pilot told me that I, too, was a pilot, and I began to push out the narrow margins of my knowledge. I learned to fly at night. I won a commercial license. In so doing I began to tread the long road toward flight by instruments through the clouds which had brought me to this high place, riding the wind, alone in the deep sky.

In silence I had striven. The more my skills expanded, the more secretive I became. I was Jekyll and I was Hyde, the black cat and the white cat, a dual personality, to the world a mining engineer of settled habits, yet of vaguely explained absences. Some people said I had changed. Perhaps I had because I had emigrated to a far country where they could not follow—that other country of the sky which was all about them and affected their lives profoundly yet which they could not see, which they saw every day yet could not know. Occasionally they were my guests in the sky. I drew the curtain back a little for them. My gift to them was a glimpse of that far country. With the secrecy of a moth forming in a chrysalis, I had grown as a pilot. Now I was an instrument pilot, albeit a new one; but the chrysalis had torn open, and a new moth had taken wing.

Was it all worth it? Oh yes, it was worth anything and everything, heaped full, piled up, and a thousand times over. Because what can be dearer than that which is dearly bought?

2

The Dream

To fly through the air with the greatest of ease—what a cry from the heart! What utter longing down through all the ages of mankind! What yearnings those words speak for us now! How we have striven, what dangers we have faced, how much human life has been spent to make it come true, to achieve flight!

Ask what single invention, if any, proves that mankind is more than a crew of inquisitive, tinkering, nifty-fingered apes. I'll tell you: Mastery of the miracle of flight. The airplane was not a development of something which went before, as was the locomotive. Nor did it come solely from observation, in the way that the greatest of steel ships derives ultimately from a log floating in the water. Though inspired by bird flight, it did not come from the observation of that flight, because all flying creatures flap their wings. Yet ornithopters have never worked, and flight by this means has hitherto eluded us even though we have walked on the moon.

Human flight was the strangest thing you ever saw. It was a pure invention. It was the summation of everything we had discovered about our world, combined with our ability to predict, to design, to engineer. Until our store of knowledge was great enough, until our ability to pull a concept out of thin air and give it form had sufficiently advanced, we could not fly.

For all too many of us, "to fly through the air with the greatest of ease" has shrunk in meaning to the middle seat of a jumbo jet on a long night flight. No, that is not what is meant at all. The longing in those words is not to be flown by someone else and to be content with those glimpses of the sky granted by the whims of airline ticket agents. It is to fly ourselves whither we will, when we will, to come and go through

6

the air of our own volition, to go somewhere or to go nowhere but up there.

Yet even our speech affirms how utterly earthbound we are. "He has both feet on the ground" translates to, "He is a sane person of mature judgment." By contrast, if "he doesn't know which way is up," he is incapable of guiding his own affairs. Ask an aerobatic pilot which way is up! "He has his head in the clouds" or "He's on cloud nine" disparages a person as being out of touch with reality. Finally, "What a bird-brain!" "What a person of minuscule intelligence!"

Truly I tell you, it is a strange road, always long and often hard, of awe and of mystery, with moments of sheer terror and gnawing fears and doubts, yet of piercing beauty, of peace and of joy, to become a pilot, to fly through the air with the greatest of ease.

A common misconception, among others that cause people to ask the weirdest questions, runs: "Private pilot license in six months and the freedom of the skies is mine." A kindred myth, not unsupported by some aircraft manufacturers and certain books of 1960s vintage, states: "In six months you could be flying your own personal airliner." It soon dawns on the aspiring pilot that flying is not as easy as it looks, and that in many weather conditions the freedom of the sky is about as desirable as the freedom of some of the nastier parts of a big city on a Saturday night.

An essential fact not always realized by ground-bound people is that there are two basic modes of flight: visual and instrument. In visual flight the pilot keeps the aircraft upright and on course by looking outside at the ground. A small aircraft flying on a sunny day is in visual meteorological conditions (VMC) and operating under the visual flight rules (VFR). When cloud or darkness intervenes to make the ground reference and landmarks invisible, control and navigation can be maintained only by means of gyroscopic, pressure-sensing, electronic, and other instruments inside the aircraft. The degree of equipment and pilot training required is much higher. An aircraft flying through cloud is in instrument meteorological conditions (IMC) and operating under the instrument flight rules (IFR). Much flight under IFR is conducted in clear air above or between cloud layers, or indeed in sight of the ground, to the extent that comparatively little time may be spent actually in cloud. Visual flight continued into instrument conditions, however, is generally of brief duration and attended by fatal results.

The Canadian private pilot license, pure and simple, allows the holder to fly in day visual conditions only. Visual flying at night requires further training and an endorsement to the license. Instrument flying, whether in the United States or Canada, requires an instrument rating, which involves more training in itself than did the private license from the beginning. Restriction to visual flight in daylight seriously limits the usefulness of the aircraft as a means of transport. High winds also pose a problem for the light-plane pilot because of turbulence near the ground. The ability to handle the aircraft in high winds is a skill acquired only through practice (for a small aircraft 25 knots [30 mph] may be considered a high wind). The American private pilot license includes training in night visual flying, and U.S. regulations allow visual flight above cloud decks ("VFR on top"), which Canadian regulations do not.

Looking in my diary for my first two years of flight, I find that the chances of completing a predetermined flight under VFR on a predetermined date were no better than 50%. These chances were somewhat better in summer and almost nil in winter. An experienced pilot flying over a known route could improve those odds, although some have come to grief trying to do so. In fairness it must be said that this applies to the Pacific Northwest, which, being mountainous, offers a variety of adverse weather conditions. Over flatter country in a drier climate, the odds would be better. The fact remains that the sky is cloudy or dark over large parts of North America for much of the time, and anyone aspiring to be a safe, proficient pilot must eventually learn to operate in such conditions.

There is attrition among flight trainees severe enough to cause concern in the aviation community. The April 1978 edition of *Flying* stated that, of those who set out to become pilots, only 40% win their wings as private pilots. Of those who do, half give up flying before they have flown 100 hours. At the Victoria Flying Club, one of the larger flying clubs and flight schools in Canada, it is reckoned that a third of those who begin flying lessons fail to reach solo flight. Of those who graduate as private pilots, 50%–60% disappear from the scene and probably never fly to any significant extent again.

This attrition is easy enough to understand. For those who never win their wings it is too difficult, too time-consuming, too expensive, or all three. Moral support may be lacking on the home front. Many of those who graduate learn to fly in summer. When summer is gone, short days and foul weather so curtail their flying that their still meager skills atrophy. They are hedged in by the restrictions of visual flying, but the road to increased capability is longer and harder than that which they have just traveled with so much difficulty. Unknown procedures away from home base intimidate them. They find it so hard to spread their wings that in the end they fold them up and tuck them away for good.

Many private pilots remain content with the pleasures of visual flight. They fly regularly enough to keep their skills in shape. They accept their limitations. When the weather is fine, they go flying. They putter about the skies on weekends and summer evenings, visit friends and relations, go to fly-ins and fly-outs, and have a super time in clear skies, in daylight, right side up.

Yet for some of us that is not enough. We are bitten by curiosity, fascinated by challenge, driven by a yearning to enhance and perfect our skills and by a demand that flight be a usable means of transport. The private pilot stands on the ground under the glory of a full moon in a clear sky and wonders why he is not flying. So he wins a night endorsement—and flies better as a result. He wonders what it is like to fly loops and rolls and Immelmanns and hammerheads. So he sneaks up on an instructor with a propensity for aerobatics and pesters him to pass on his skills—and flies better as a result. Someone takes him on an IFR flight and the unearthly beauty of cloudscapes seen from within fascinates him, along with the sheer enhancement of the light plane as a means of transport.

But he needs two to three years' worth of pilot-in-command time to qualify for an instrument rating. Someone tells him that a commercial license is but a small sidestep on the way and, sure enough, he falls for it. Once again his skills improve. When he eventually wins his coveted instrument rating after two or three years of training, he gains to some extent the freedom of the skies as a proficient pilot. Of course, it is by no means necessary to train continuously, but the process is unlikely to take less than two years.

The three most common questions are: "How safe is it?" "How easy is it?" "How expensive is it?" All are reasonable concerns.

How safe is flying in a light aircraft? An alert, healthy, well-trained, practiced pilot flying a properly maintained, commercially built aircraft and exercising proper skill and judgment in the conduct of his flight is safer than in many earthbound occupations and even some forms of recreation. But, if any of these characteristics is deficient or absent, flying can be extremely dangerous. An aircraft accident is magnified out of all proportion simply because an aircraft is involved. A fender bender caused by a botched landing becomes a "plane crash." In 1984 a light aircraft was flown into a hill in England, killing four people. It was prominently reported in a newspaper in Victoria, British Columbia, a third of the way round the world. Other events causing multiple fatalities are seldom reported outside the area in which they occur.

It is sometimes said that most pilots know someone who has been killed flying. At that the safety freaks and ground-pounders shake their heads and say how terrible it is and it shouldn't be allowed. Some cry, with nauseating self-righteousness: "I don't feel the need to do what you do. Therefore I don't see why you should be allowed to do it. I envy your skill and courage because I have neither and, when you fly overhead, it offends me. I will cause the Bureaucracy to clip your little wings so that you may never fly except in an airline seat with your brain turned off like me. That is flying." Most people of whatever age in Europe and North America know someone who was killed in a car crash. I can think of seven—one for every five years of my life—but no one ever says anything about that.

The aviation press itself presents a false picture. One magazine contains no less than two regular columns devoted to fatal accidents, some of which occurred for no apparent reason (with none offered), and one column devoted to hair-raising narrow escapes. The spirit is of honest inquiry and collective soul-searching, and the columns are of value to the flying community. But to the layman they must present a picture of endless and macabre disaster which is entirely misleading and conceals the thousands of flights going on every day that are unworthy of note simply because they are utterly uneventful, although profoundly satisfying to the participants.

The improvement of flight safety is interwoven with the development of aviation as a whole. Human flight today is a stage in an evolutionary process—the result of events past, the forerunner of others to come. "Flight safety" is nothing more than mankind's will to survive in an intensely alluring, yet potentially lethal, environment. Let us look back at the road which we have traveled.

The Wright brothers, in a feat of the utmost genius, designed a wing with predictable behavior and found a power plant that would produce enough power to overcome the effect of its own weight. They realized that the wing was unstable fore-and-aft (left to its own devices it would not fly but would tumble when passing through the air) and added a stabilizing winglet on an extension of the structure. They achieved manned flight in a machine heavier than air.

This achievement, great in itself, merely opened a Pandora's box (of which the brothers were well aware) of how to control the craft in flight. Once airborne, it was locked in a web of forces, static and dynamic, single, opposed, or combined, which has exercised the highest reaches of applied mathematics ever since. The Wright brothers' machines were marginally controllable; their characteristics in uncontrolled flight were benign, which saved the brothers' lives. Equally marginal were the nascent skills of the pilots.

The first aviators built their own aircraft, taught themselves to fly, and killed themselves in quantities in the process. Then, as now, breaking the rules carried the death penalty, but at that time no one knew what the rules were. Very little was known about how to make aircraft strong enough in the right places to withstand the loads of normal flight and of the unavoidable excursions into abnormal flight which resulted from a corresponding ignorance of control and technique. Structure, control, and pilot training were in their infancy. Flying was suicidally dangerous. We are fortunate that there were men bold enough to accept the challenge.

World War I established the flying machine as a weapon marginally more dangerous to the enemy than to its pilot. The years between the two world wars saw the development of an idea, radical at the time, that the aircraft could offer a form of transportation, either personal or public. But not until the late 1930s did airline transportation begin to approach rail travel in comfort, safety, and predictability. In that decade the aircraft underwent a startling metamorphosis from a biplane with an open cockpit and a cat's cradle of external bracing wires and struts into the sleek monoplane of today.

World War II profoundly affected all aspects of aviation. Most obvious were the improvements in structural and aerodynamic design and in engine power. The need to train unprecedented numbers of civilians to be military pilots caused a corresponding increase in the attention given to methods of instruction, a process which has continued since. The war left a legacy of experienced ex-military pilots and instructors from which civil aviation has benefited ever since. It is significant that one of the most penetrating of all expositions of airplane flight, Langewiesche's *Stick and Rudder*,* first appeared in 1944.

The aircraft commonly used for training today have in some cases been in production for thirty years, and their characteristics are

---

*W. Langewiesche, *Stick and Rudder* (New York: McGraw-Hill, 1972; original work published 1944).

known in the finest detail. First-class, highly experienced instruction is available, and it is up to the would-be pilot to find it and make the best possible use of it. These are potent safety factors.

The frontier of flight is far beyond the speed of sound, and it extends into space. How this frontier has been pushed back is told in Hallion's fascinating and scholarly work, *Test Pilots: The Frontiersmen of Flight*.* Like all frontiers, this frontier has its dangers, but the modern light aircraft is in well-known territory. The new pilot's frontier is his own skill and judgment. If he learns, studies, and flies diligently and with due caution, but not without courage, his flying will be as safe as anything can reasonably be. If he neglects these things, or otherwise adapts poorly to flight, he risks being weeded out in the ruthless process of natural selection.

Fear of flight is a common problem in itself and is a reaction to dangers that are perceived rather than actual. Flight arouses deep, irrational fears. Some people are scared of flying in airliners but not in small planes, or vice versa, or both. Fear of flight is a variation on the fear of heights and open spaces. It is perfectly natural to be alarmed at being given control of an unfamiliar, unpredictable, self-willed, noisy object charging at high speed through thin air in response to an arcane internal logic. Most of us, however, can eventually bring our fears under control, enjoy the triumph of staring them down, and then use them as servants to warn us of danger, not as masters to keep us on the ground. These fears gradually evaporate as we accept the reality of flight deep within ourselves and our ability to exert total control over it.

How easy is flying? Flying within the limitations of training and equipment and in suitable weather conditions is very easy. Learning to fly—expanding those limitations—is not. Anyone who says it is should be regarded with suspicion. Many such people started as military pilots. It follows that they possessed a high degree of natural aptitude and underwent intensive full-time training at someone else's expense. For the civilian student pilot the demands on spare time, money, and energy are colossal, but so are the eventual rewards.

Most student pilots are attacked by the thought, "If other people find it so easy, why do I find it so difficult? I must be in some way deficient." This thought is both destructive and unnecessary. Learning to fly is a challenge—always has been, always will be. In a world of the

---

* R.P. Hallion, *Test Pilots: The Frontiersmen of Flight* (Washington: Smithsonian Institution, 1989).

quick-and-easy, flying is neither. Indeed, some people conditioned to the push-button security of urban life show a terrifying lack of common sense when exposed to the realities of flight. But let the most cocooned city dweller bemoan the lack of adventure in an artificial world. All that he or she must do is go to the nearest of airfields and Places Where They Fly, discover the surreal beauty of the wild sky, and be initiated into the mystery of flight.

Flying comes easily to some, less so to others. It comes most easily to the sixteen-to-twenty age group, increasing in difficulty with increasing age. What is unpredictable, and often surprising, is which aspects of flight come most easily to which people. I found the initial (private pilot) stage appallingly difficult; it took every scrap of courage and determination to battle through with it. Night flying came more easily. Instrument flying was lots of hard work, but I never found flight in actual instrument conditions to be a problem. Basic aerobatics were a breeze. Yet one aerobatic pilot never had the self-confidence to solo at night. Some proficient pilots cannot fly aerobatics even if they wish to. Some good visual pilots have difficulty learning to fly by instruments. Everyone has trouble with something. The only question is what.

People often ask, "Isn't it rather expensive?" I reply, "Yes, but plenty of people spend a lot more money on things that do them a lot less good." Most boat owners could afford an aircraft instead if they were so minded. The training for a private license costs as much as a holiday to somewhere exotic. After the vacation is over, you have a stack of bills, a fading suntan, and "this-is-us-on-Waikiki-Beach-but-it-didn't-turn-out-too-good." After you have a private pilot license. . . .

Plenty of golf and country clubs charge initiation fees that would cover the cost of training for private and commercial licenses and the instrument rating. My nephew bought himself a music synthesizer; he could have learned to fly for the same price. From discovery ride to instrument rating, three years of almost continuous flight training cost me about as much as a new medium-sized car, except that flight training was pay-as-you-go, some of it was deductible against income tax, and. . . . Well, it's a question of priorities.

What is this creature, this "airplane"? Airplanes are so diverse that in some cases the only resemblance between them is that they fly. We can, however, zoom in on the kind on which we, as civilian student pilots, will focus our attention (not to mention care, affection, fear, bewilderment, frustration, and abuse, at various times). It is the single-engined, land-based, light aircraft.

It is an "aircraft" because it is a craft of the air, traveling through the air without visible support. Our minds are conditioned from birth that what cannot be seen is not there. Remember your rage and fright the last time you walked into something you did not see? Every solid object is attached to the ground or supported by or hung from something . . . that is, except for a flying creature. Next time you see a bird or an aircraft in flight, look at the invisible air all around it and watch it fly.

The light aircraft is so called because it weighs a ton or less. As a result, it is easily blown about by the wind and bounced up and down by turbulence which airline passengers seldom feel.

It has one engine because that is all that most of us can afford, all that we need, and all that our brains can take in. Contrary to common supposition, two engines are not always safer than one. Beneath its glossy exterior an aircraft with two engines conceals a mare's nest of unsuspected complexities. When things go wrong, they can do so rapidly and in large numbers so that all the skills of a professional pilot and co-pilot are needed to keep the flight under control. Sometimes even that is not enough. Statistics show that the twin-engined aircraft allows the part-time pilot to fly himself into situations which he can handle only when everything, including the weather, is functioning according to plan—an insecure premise.

The natural question which people ask about single-engined aircraft is: "What happens if the engine quits?" Good maintenance and piloting can reduce this risk to the level of the more bizarre natural hazards, such as being struck by lightning, and far below that of being involved in a road accident. The American National Transportation Safety Board found that Cessna 172 aircraft suffered damage from the results of unavoidable engine failure once every 303,448 hours—equivalent to thirty-five years of continuous round-the-clock flight. Of these, 5% resulted in fatalities. The average private pilot flies 50–100 hours per year. An aircraft rental company with ten aircraft may fly 500–700 hours in a good month. A pilot with 20,000 hours will be near the end of a lifetime of professional flying.

People have been landing aircraft without engine power ever since the earliest days of flight. Sailplane pilots do it all the time. From 5,000 feet above the ground, in still air, the average light aircraft will glide 10 miles in any direction. You are not going to fly your single-engined aircraft for any significant length of time outside gliding distance from some sort of forced landing ground (are you?). You would be surprised how plentiful forced landing grounds are when you are looking down from 5,000 feet. At the worst, a ton of aircraft landing at 50 knots is not very fussy about what it lands on or in. Then, too, you are going to be a hot pilot with all your operating and emergency procedures wired (aren't you?).

Consider a car engine, used roughly with incessant changes of speed and torque and little or no maintenance, subjected to fierce vibration, bombarded with stones, mud, and dust, built to lower standards than an aero engine and fed with lower-grade, sometimes contaminated, fuels and lubricants, and how often does it fail without warning? If you are still worried about engine failure, just stay on the ground—while I go flying.

For a generalization, there are three kinds of light aircraft: two-seat, four-seat, and "sophisticated." In the beginning all aircraft were "light aircraft," but the light plane as we know it began to appear in the 1930s as a single-engined, fixed-undercarriage (landing gear), monoplane with a cloth-covered structure. The decade after 1945 brought forth a rich variety of light aircraft with all-metal structures and tricycle undercarriages for better ground handling, and the first light aircraft for private use in significant numbers with retractable undercarriages. Some of these designs have continued in production with minor modifications for thirty years. The proliferation of radio navigation aids and the advent of, first, the transistor and, then, the microcomputer have combined to give the light aircraft capabilities which even military aircraft and airliners did not possess in 1950. Whether the private pilot is able or willing to handle the cost and complexity of these "avionics" is another question.

The two-seater is the cheapest to buy and operate and, as such, is typically used for training, local pleasure flying, and some traveling. It will carry two people and about as much baggage as you can pick up with one hand, as well as its fuel. It flies at 100 mph with a 100-hp engine. It has wheels on stalks underneath for moving about on the ground. Examples presently in use are the Cessna 150 and 152, Piper Tomahawk, and Beech Skipper. Cessna, Piper, and Beech have been the big three in light aircraft manufacturing, although this situation is changing.

The four-seaters are heavier, slightly faster, and more comfortable on a long flight. Being roomier inside, they can accommodate more baggage and radio equipment. Being heavier, they are more stable in turbulence. Typically they have an engine of 150–180 hp and cruise at 125 mph. Examples are the Cessna 172, Piper Cherokee and its derivatives, and Beech Musketeer.

"Sophisticated" light aircraft carry four to six people. The wheels may retract into the wings or fuselage in flight to reduce air resistance and so allow the aircraft to fly faster. A "constant-speed propeller" is used to improve engine efficiency and, hence, speed. Engines range in size from 180 to 250 hp, and cruising speeds are in the 150–200 mph bracket. Examples are the Cessna 182, Piper Comanche and its derivatives, Beech Bonanza, the Mooney series of aircraft, and some others. Sophistication, speed, and power carry a heavy price tag and place additional demands on the pilot.

Chances are that you will learn to fly in a two-seater, and, more likely than not, it will be a Cessna 152. But the quality of instruction and the efficiency of the training organizations are more important than the type of aircraft they fly. "Buy it and fly it" is attractive but impractical. Learning to fly is enough of a challenge without worrying about maintaining and licensing the aircraft as well.

But enough of this! How do you learn to fly? Above all, what is it really like?

3

Why?

One bright morning in the early 1950s a Lockheed Constellation flew its unhurried approach over the suburbs of London into Heathrow airport. The thick growl of its four engines reached down into narrow streets and walled gardens. A child looked up at the spreading silver wings so close above and saw, for the first time, an airplane.

World War II had ended less than a decade before. My father had been an air gunner with RAF Bomber Command. In that distant era known as "before the war," my mother had grieved for a beau who flew small airplanes. His aircraft had spun and crashed. Mine was not a "flying family," but flight had impinged on us in no small way.

At the Farnborough Airshow in 1960, breaking the sound barrier was still quite a new achievement and the English Electric Lightning was the hottest thing in the sky. Back in 1918 the hottest thing in the sky had been a biplane fighter called the SE-5. Flown and cared for by loving hands, it could still, in 1960, walk tall in front of the million-dollar monsters with their blazing afterburners and sonic bangs and quietly steal the show. It fired its Lewis gun into the ground; the puffs of dust showed that it was not firing blanks either. Climbing up again, it gyrated a few times in a gentle spin and flew unconcernedly away.

One warm Saturday afternoon, on leave from a Northamptonshire boarding school, we visited a small grass airfield called Sywell. Little airplanes sprang into the air one by one, or swooped down to land. Farnborough was the unattainable sophistication of military flying, but at Sywell ordinary mortals were taking to the air. I made a promise that one day I, too, would spring into the air.

At a boys' boarding school in the 1960s, flight was The Big Deal. Our heroes were the wartime military aircrew and the early supersonic test pilots. The school had an enormous hall with a polished hardwood floor. It was a common practice to apply maximum thrust at one end, only to reach the other with smoking brakes and a feeling of disappointment at not having lifted off. In the evenings we flew along the upstairs corridor and turned in through the dormitory door, doing about 130 knots on final approach to a carrier deck landing, to be received by an arrester wire made of knotted neckties. This did nothing for the neckties and was forbidden accordingly. Paper airplanes were even more strictly forbidden, but no legal paper dart ever flew loops, chandelles, and barrel rolls like those we so furtively enjoyed.

The school abounded with Frog, Revell, and Airfix models of Spitfires and Lancasters in varying stages of construction and destruction. Some people spent hours of thought on what would now be called an ultralight, although with no idea of what would happen once they were airborne. The trouble was that we were two-dimensional ground-pounders down here while our pilotless creations glided and looped and stalled up there, and never the twain could meet. Only the V-bombers, drawing their vapor trails across the blue sky, knew the answer.

We knew what it was like from the memoirs of the wartime fighter pilots as they stall-turned out of the sun and followed their opponents in graying-out turns. Of course we knew what it was like. The aircraft books were dog-eared where they described the latest jet fighters, but no one spared a second glance for a two-seat Cessna. Those things could fly at only 100 mph. They were only once removed from the plastic kits that came in a polyethylene bag with a capsule of glue and cost half-a-crown.

Once I made a crude object, shaped not unlike a Spitfire, from the stiff card backs of used-up exercise books. It flew. It glided for 10 feet across the floor. I snipped the wings at the trailing edge and gave it flaps. Bend the flaps up and it would go up—any fool knew that. It didn't. It smacked straight into the floor. Bend the flaps down and it would nose-dive. Not a bit of it. A small deflection made it glide further. Therefore, with a larger deflection it should glide better still. Wrong again! With a vague feeling that things were not as they seemed, I dismissed it as a fluke. Enmeshed in the grimmer and duller realities of growing up, and spoiling my eyesight with the enforced study of dead languages, I abandoned all thought of flight for twenty years.

Flight did not quite abandon me. At the age of sixteen, I piloted a small airplane, belonging to friends, across the skies of Wales—for about ten minutes. That is to say, I sat rigid at the controls and interfered as little as possible with the benign wishes of the aircraft until a thermal surprised it and it did not know what to do. Neither did I, and the owner's practiced hand calmed it down. In the cramped conditions of England, where everything is more or less restricted, flying is for the military, the airlines, and a few rich eccentrics. Otherwise there is no money, no room, no airfields. Besides, the weather is unspeakable and the cost unbelievable.

A career as a mining engineer took me to the broad skies and more generous lifestyle of North America. For six years I lived in bleak, tough little mining towns in various parts of the continent, but eventually, in 1982, the dice came up sixes with a tunneling job in the island paradise of Victoria, British Columbia. My employer had piloted his own plane and, when he knew of my intentions, gave me every encouragement to go and fly. I had never been able to justify the cost solely for recreation, but there seemed to be some likelihood that flying might be a useful adjunct to my career. The pieces of the puzzle fell into place.

For months through the winter I devoured the aviation section of the local library to find out what I was getting into. I felt that I knew so much about it that I could almost step into an airplane and fly. I was going to learn fast and well. I had flown in airliners and was not scared. I was ready and loaded for bear. But there was one little thing I missed— the RAF motto *Per Ardua ad Astra.*

One problem was that no one seemed to know anyone in the flight training business. I would have to go to strangers and ask them to teach me to fly. The consensus of available opinion was that the Victoria Flying Club was The Place. I had visions of a lounge full of Pilots in deep leather armchairs with nothing to do but wait for some sprog to walk in through the door so they could laugh him to scorn. I curled up in fright at the thought.

My home was in Sooke, beyond the farthest western limits of Victoria. The airport was at Sidney, thirty miles away by road, beyond the northernmost outskirts of the city. One Sunday afternoon I drove out there and stopped on a low hill overlooking the airfield. A flock of small airplanes was taking off, circling about, landing, and forthwith taking off again—"touch-and-go landings." Flying around the field looked simple enough, even dull. In fact most of the maneuvers in the how-to-fly books seemed like that. I absorbed the atmosphere for a while and returned to Sooke.

No amount of armchair flying would produce results. I would have to grasp the nettle. What for, anyway? To follow a star? To chase the end of the rainbow? To keep a promise? Or to fly through the air with the greatest of ease? The truth was that I had cold feet. Freedom of action is also freedom of inaction, so nothing happened for a time.

Spring comes early to Vancouver Island. On the first warm Sunday morning of the year, I was standing in my back doorway enjoying the scenery of the Sooke Basin. A fluttery noise made me look up. It was a silver Ercoupe pointing straight at me in a shallow dive. Barely 300 feet overhead, the pilot poured on the power and climbed away. I don't know if the pilot was even aware of a man standing in a doorway looking at him, but he certainly produced results. If that was not a Sign from the Sky, it would do until one came along. I made tracks for the airport that same afternoon.

4

Discovery Ride

The Victoria Flying Club was cleverly hidden in the airport industrial area under the watchful eye of the control tower. I parked my Chev at a distance and approached stealthily on foot, antennae fully extended. It was a busy afternoon, and a stream of small airplanes trundled out to the runway. One by one they revved their engines with the snarls of angry terriers and hurled themselves into the sky.

Something inside me suddenly rebelled: "Tom Morrison, are you actually presuming that you will climb into one of those frail craft and launch yourself into the air? Even that such a thing could happen today, forthwith? Enough of this foolishness! Your ground-bound self is entirely adequate to the normal purposes of existence. Now turn your back on this business and confine yourself to armchair flying like everyone else." I turned away in an agony of indecision. But a man has to be able to look himself in the eye.

A sign outside the Flying Club building read: "Cessna Pilot Center: Discover Flying." That looked reassuring. A flying school: You go to school, you learn certain things in a specified length of time, you emerge with certain skills. Learn to drive; learn to fly. But "Flying School"? What a misleading expression! Flight is to be approached with prayer and fasting and knightly vigil, because to take active control of an aircraft in flight is to cross the threshold of a new life. Nothing will ever be the same again. There are two kinds of people: those who have and those who have not. "Flying School"?: a most misleading expression.

A cat burglar in a haunted house could have taken deportment lessons from me as I entered the Flying Club building and crept along a quiet corridor. Offset from the end of the corridor was a room with an L-shaped counter in the middle. Behind the counter stood a man who was obviously a middle-aged country doctor, complete with tweed jacket, tie, and spectacles. His stethoscope would be in a bulgy pocket. He observed my entry. I addressed him, viz.: "I'm interested in learning to fly"—a lead-off calculated to contain the right admixture of inquiry and stated intent. The doctor raised his eyebrows in mild amusement: "Oh yes?" We eyed each other long enough for me to ascertain that nothing further was forthcoming. I followed through: "Could you point me at someone who will help me?" The doctor beckoned a strikingly beautiful girl from behind a desk, who asked me a number of searching questions while he betook himself to more pressing affairs.

Step #1 was a "discovery flight," which was the opportunity to discover whether to go ahead, the final opportunity for cold feet to triumph. No discovery flights were available for three quarters of an hour. I think they tell everybody that to see if they come back or not. At five minutes to three I was back.

Outside, on the flight line, the doctor was inspecting a red and white Cessna 152. The Cessna 150/152 have probably taught more people to fly than any aircraft since the Tigermoth and the Piper Cub. It is at once rugged, gentle, and forgiving. It misbehaves only when forced to, and then after much protest. Its only conceivable defect is that it is not airplane-shaped. Look at it! A Cub, a Cherokee, an Ercoupe, they are all airplane-shaped. But a Cessna 150? No sir. Someone took a wing, a good, hefty, no-nonsense wing. He hung a fuselage under it with no apparent support. He gave the fuselage two ends. The pointy end has a little matchstick propeller; a fashion-conscious designer put a swept fin on the other end, giving the aircraft a faintly dissolute appearance. Then he put stalks with wheels under the fuselage. Finally he wound it up and it flew away. When it got tired, it came back and asked him to wind it up again so it could fly some more. It has been teaching people to fly ever since.

The doctor led me through a detailed external inspection to make sure that all the pieces were in their rightful places. I eyed the airplane with extreme suspicion. It might bite. We dipsticked the fuel tanks and oil sump, and drew fuel from the drain valves. We went all around the aircraft checking vents and cotter pins and hinges—in all about eighty items. We climbed in, the doctor in the right seat, myself in the left (hot) seat. The craft had only two seats with precious little room for two full-sized men. Even the control yoke seemed minute. We slammed the doors with a tinny snap. The whole affair seemed very insubstantial.

The doctor whipped out a printed checklist and manipulated some of the knobs and switches. Master switch ON—CLUNK! I jumped. Something ran up to speed with a whine. The engine started with a cough and a roar. The aircraft shook itself like a dog. The doctor twiddled some knobs on the radio set, which caused a peroration sounding like a recital in some obscure foreign language to come through a loudspeaker in the cabin roof. More work on the knobs and switches, and the aircraft was alive and quivering, eager to bear its nervous passenger aloft.

We could talk to the control tower on a two-way radio by using a microphone which lived on a hook below the instrument panel when not in use. When the tower talked back, it came out through the loudspeaker in the cabin roof. The tower directed us to runway 26, and we taxied out. I expressed admiration that anyone could find his way about on a featureless airfield. This feeble witticism produced only a fraction of the disdain it deserved.

As we trundled along the taxiway, I went through my own mental checklist:

Mouth—SHUT & DRY
Breathing—NORMAL
Adrenaline glands—ACTIVATE
Heart rate—MAXIMUM
Brain—DISENGAGE
Sanity—CHECK DEFICIENT

There is a difference between riding in an aircraft as a passenger and doing so for the future purpose of controlling its path through the sky. Maybe it would be simpler to pay someone else to do the flying and leave it at that.

We stopped by the runway while the doctor ran the engine up to make sure the plane was ready for flight. It seemed that a Boeing 747 departing for Europe could hardly receive a more intensive checkout than this.

Takeoff clearance came over the radio. (I had always thought it was those red lights beside the runway.) We taxied out onto the runway. The throttle was a knob sticking out of the lower part of the instrument panel. The doctor gently pushed it all the way in to apply full power. With a throaty roar from the engine, we ate up the asphalt and soon slid off into the air. I had watched the ground fall away beneath an airliner, but, in this eggbox hanging under a wing, it was different. It was a long way down, and I was not sure that I wanted to be where I was, not at all sure. Then we were over the water of Patricia Bay, and it felt even worse.

We climbed away to the south toward Victoria. Beneath us lay a tangle of forested hills and a few lakes. Already I was utterly lost. At the doctor's bidding I took hold of the yoke, firmly in both hands. To my surprise the controls were springy to the touch. Nothing was quite as it seemed it should be. No single action on the controls had any single effect. Backward pressure on the yoke made the aircraft climb, but the airspeed decreased as shown on the instrument with the white needle and the green and yellow arcs. Forward pressure made the aircraft go down, and the airspeed increased. Open the throttle, and the nose would rise up and yaw left *and* the airspeed would decrease, not increase as one might suppose. Tip the aircraft sideways to the left, and it would turn left. But gentle toe pressure on the right rudder pedal would level the wings and at the same time stop the turn. It was all so paradoxical.

In front of me was a panel full of instruments with colored arcs and segments, needles, and symbols of hidden meaning. When the aircraft hung in space in level flight, they seemed asleep, yet their very stillness spoke in an unknown language. As the aircraft changed its posture, they all moved in apparent disharmony. Through these instruments, by what I could see outside, and by the sounds of the engine and of the wind of our passage, the aircraft's flight was described to me in every detail. Yet I understood none of it. In seeing I saw not; in hearing I heard not; in feeling I felt not; in this incomprehension lurked fear.

After allowing me to savor the strangeness of it all, the doctor demonstrated some tight turns in which the aircraft seemed to stand on its wingtip, and then it was time to return to base. There was more baffling communion between the doctor and the oracles in the control tower. He extended the flaps into the rumbling slipstream; the runway came up toward us; he let the aircraft settle onto the ground so lightly that I had to look out of the side window to see if we had, in fact, landed.

We taxied in and switched off. The thick silence was broken only by the ticking of the engine as it cooled. I asked the doctor if he thought I was pilot material. He was noncommittal. To him flying a small airplane was as normal as walking about. The gist of his reply was: "If you want to do it, do it. If you don't want to do it, don't do it." He added: "If you're nervous, don't do it." I was good and nervous, but I had done plenty of things which had at first frightened me, some of them dangerous. I said that I had enjoyed every minute of the flight. My decision point was long past.

We disentangled ourselves from the little airplane and went into the room with the counter. This was the moment of public affirmation, whether to sign up for flying lessons. After a discovery flight you pay your $20 and, if you wish, you can walk away with no questions asked, without even knowing the name of the instructor with whom you flew. But, when the pupil books the first flying lesson, there is an unspoken commitment both ways, and a deep one. The instructor agrees to take on a pupil (or acolyte). The acolyte agrees to submit to the demands and discipline of flight training. There is no song and dance about it, but it exists nonetheless.

The doctor's name was Doug MacColl. We looked each other up and down briefly. I said, "Well, if you think it's a good idea, I think it's a good idea." We shook hands on it. I had just shaken hands with one of the best instructors in the business. I hoped he didn't notice the sweat from my palms, which was surely leaving pools on the floor.

5

Sprog

A week after the discovery ride I met with Doug MacColl for my first real flying lesson. The sky was full of puffy clouds. The girl behind the desk said, "It'll be quite bumpy, but you don't mind, do you?" (Mind?! No, pretty wench, I don't "mind"—just like you wouldn't "mind" an evening with Count Dracula!) Doug sent me to do the walk-around check on the red and white aircraft with the registration letters C-GZLG on its side. It was referred to as ZLG in face-to-face speech and "Zulu Lima Golf" in the phonetic alphabet over the radio. Not a rivet escaped my attention, and already I was nervous. To be nervous about a parked aircraft is a well-developed case indeed.

We wound ourselves around the wing struts and fitted ourselves into the tiny cabin. I followed the checklist through the startup procedure and tuned in the foreign poetry as a new recital began.:

> This-is-Victoria-International-Airport-atis-information-kilo. The-twenty-three-hundred-zulu-weather-is-four-thousand-scattered-eight-thousand-broken-estimated-ceiling-fifteen-thousand-broken-twenty-five-thousand-thin-broken-visibility-thirty-five-miles-temperature-fifteen-dewpoint-eight-altimeter-two-niner-eight-four-wind-one-four-zero-at-ten. IFR-approach-is-radar-vectored-ILSDME-zero-eight-landings-and-departures-runway-thirteen. Inform-Victoria-ATC-on-initial-contact-that-you-have-received-information-kilo.

I turned to Doug and made the simple inquiry in a squeak beyond the auditory range of most humans: *"Whaat?"* We let the poet do his stuff for a few more minutes while I tried to interpret some small fraction of what he was saying. I discovered later that most of this had very little bearing on a local flight in a Cessna 152.

A few more knobs and switches, and we were ready. Doug told me what to say on the radio to ground control. Even taxiing poses problems for the novice. A Cessna 152 on the ground is steered with the feet. The rudder pedals are connected to the nosewheel by spring linkages. The resemblance of the control yoke to the steering wheel of a car is irresistible. But turning the yoke merely moves the ailerons, and the novice is apt to find himself heading for the weeds fanning air with the ailerons but having no influence on the aircraft's path.

Doug sat patiently while we snaked our way out to runway 13, imitating bird flight with the ailerons from time to time. Next came the problem of turning into wind to cool the engine during the run-up. Finding us about to mow the grass, I stamped on the toe brakes and let out the immortal phrase: "You have control!" *In extenso* it meant: "You are holding this thing because I am not. I have two left feet; my brain is out of order. If you don't rescue me, we will end up cutting clods." The question loomed large in my mind: "If you can't control the aircraft on the ground, how will you ever do so in the air?"

Doug whisked the airplane around, and we started the run-up. I read off each item from the checklist in a loud, quavering voice. I could hardly have been more nervous if one of the switches had been wired to a grenade. The engine bellowed eagerly. The aircraft strained against the brakes and danced in its own prop wash, as though longing to fly. Throttle to idle: run-up complete.

Another turn brought us to the runway's edge looking up the approach path. My timorous report to the control tower that we were ready for takeoff (or blast-off to the moon, or such) brought a deluge from the tower in reply: "Zulu-Lima-Golf-cleared-takeoff-right-turn-through-a-thousand-the-tower-on-nineteen-one-no-delay-please-traffic-on-final." Doug took control while I pondered this utterance, and we were airborne.

No sooner were we "safely" ensconced in the aircraft's familiar habitat than Doug told me to take control. I succeeded in continuing the climb, skidding around a right turn and avoiding the hill south of the airfield. As we climbed over the water, I felt a stab of panic and decided not to look down. It was obvious that there was nothing but fresh air a short distance under my posterior, no visible reason why we should not plunge into the brine, and no certain indication that we were not about to do so. We leveled off at the terrifying height of 2,000 feet.

The weather was showery and the air rough. Gray cloud bellies slid by over our heads. Raindrops pinged against the windshield as we flew through the showers which washed the spring landscape. Having ridden in heavy aircraft, it did not occur to me that a light aircraft would move about bodily with the air currents. I had always been afraid of heights. Two thousand feet in a craft as insubstantial as an eggbox was plenty of height to be afraid of in still air. When the thing kept falling off its perch at intervals, it was The Absolute End.

Two main considerations dominated the scene. For one thing, I was about to shell out $58 for an hour of being frightened. I was almost resolved to admit that this was not for me. For another, it matters not who a man is or thinks he is in the eyes of God, himself, and other ground-pounders. In the presence of the sky and the airplane and in the eyes of his instructor, a sprog pilot is a sprog pilot.

As a mining engineer, it had been my business to lead crews of rough diamonds in a dangerous industry in the back lots of North America. I had acquired the savvy to bear that responsibility, and the authority and self-reliance which go with it. More often than not it was my job to tell people what the score was. But now I was as helpless as a newborn child. I entrusted my life to a stranger and revealed that helplessness to him. I was thoroughly frightened while knowing that my fears were groundless. A sprog pilot is a sprog pilot.

Doug taught me how to fly straight and level, followed by some gentle turns, and how to climb and descend, as we cruised about the practice area near Duncan. If the airspeed dropped below a healthy 80 knots, I became anxious that the aircraft would stop flying and head earthward like a brick. If the angle of bank exceeded 15°, even briefly, I was scared that some appalling gyration would result. The hills around the Cowichan Valley rise to 3,000 and 4,000 feet and, if one of them loomed ahead less than five miles away, I was not happy until we had turned away from it.

At last Doug took control, and I sat back in relief as we returned to the airport. We tuned the radio to the foreign verse, to make sure that the airfield had not blown away in our absence, and went through the baffling exchange with the control tower which is appropriate at such times. It sounded like a foreign language; it came through a mediocre loudspeaker through engine and slipstream noise. It obviously was vital that I should understand what was being said, but at the same time it was impossible to do so. Learning the radio procedures was as much of a task as learning to fly the airplane.

We piped up: "Victoria Tower, Cessna 152 Golf Zulu Lima Golf,

Cowichan Bay, two thousand feet, landing with kilo."

The voice replied: "Zulu-Lima-Golf-report-over-Deep-Cove-on-one-nineteen-seven-for-a-right-base-on-thirteen."

We flew down the bay with Saltspring Island off our left wingtip. Throttled back and losing height, we went over Deep Cove at 1,000 feet, changed the radio frequency to 119.7 MHz, and reported to the tower again. This time it was even worse: "Zulu-Lima-Golf-cleared-to-a-right-base-on-thirteen-number-one-on-thirteen-number-two-to-land-traffic-is-a-Cessna-four-oh-two-final-on-zero-eight."

We swung in over a swath cut through the trees, which led to a black runway. Doug pointed out that, because there was a slight crosswind, we would have to sideslip to keep lined up with the runway. The wind was blowing us sideways one way, and we had to fly sideways at the same rate in the opposite direction? The list of difficulties that had not occurred to me was growing by the minute. Doug eased the aircraft onto the runway with the faintest bump, and my first flying lesson was over. I felt wrung out. Another week would pass before I put my nerves to the test again.

In due time I learned to hold the yoke in my left hand, leaving my right hand for a surprising variety of other tasks—throttle, carburetor heat, mixture control, flaps, lights, trim, and radio.

Doug took a well-earned vacation and I found myself flying with Derek, who was about my own age. Doug greeted his pupils with a broad grin and the almost unvarying: "Up, up, and *away* we go!" So we climbed in and went. Derek had taken his instructor's course more recently (about thirty years more recently), and each lesson started with a briefing, which gave my apprehensions time to develop full strength. Doug's training flights were conducted at any suitable altitude, airspeed, and direction of flight. If Derek said 67 knots, he meant 67 knots, and other figures to match.

Derek demanded more and pushed more into me. I liked it at first, but it concealed a serious disadvantage: Although flying by exact numbers is at times praiseworthy and at times downright essential, the source of those numbers is the instrument panel. The natural result can be an absurd state of affairs whereby the new student pilot flies the aircraft by the instruments instead of by using his normal senses, admiring the view, and keeping a sharp lookout for other aircraft. Plenty of flying has been done, and still is, in aircraft which do not have any instruments. The student can also pile up tension by chasing numbers which at that stage are unimportant in comparison to the overall job of controlling the aircraft.

On our first flight I was keen to impress Derek with my conscientiousness and competence as far as it went. I could happily have spent the time absorbing the sensation of flight as we cruised over the hills of Saltspring Island. But Derek thought that some of the next lesson should be pushed into my numb skull, and demonstrated a stall. The stall warning let out its spooky whine, and the aircraft quit sitting on whatever it had been sitting on and dropped like a brick. But why spoil a perfectly good flight on a fine spring afternoon with a dumb thing like a stall?

The idea crept up on me that instructors are maniacs hell-bent on distorting the normal perceptions of which way is up and which way down, for whom no flight is complete without a wide variety of simulated emergencies—engine failure, radio failure, fire, spiral dives, stalls, spins, and the rest. Where is the joy of flight if the pilot must be forever anticipating these things? The answer is that the joy of flight lies in a reasonable certainty of being able to prevent such emergencies from happening in the first place and of being able to handle them if they do occur.

The next lesson was with Doug. We concentrated on turns at 30° and 45° of bank. This is not a textbook, and there are plenty of good books which explain how an aircraft turns. Suffice it to say that if you tip an airplane to one side, it will turn in the same direction. The more steeply you tilt it, the more rapidly it will turn. In light plane flying there are gentle, medium, and steep turns, at 15°, 30°, and 45°, respectively, of bank. As soon as the aircraft is tipped on its side, it wants to descend, or if climbing, to climb less steeply. It also wants either to level its wings or to roll into a steeper bank, depending both on the angle of bank and whether the turn is level, climbing, or descending. The steeper the bank, the more forcefully it expresses its wishes.

Doug demonstrated an alarming maneuver called a spiral dive, which can result from a steep turn gone wrong, and which is also a natural tendency of some aircraft when left to their own devices. If the pilot does nothing but haul back on the yoke in an attempt to raise the nose, the aircraft winds into a steeper and tighter downward spiral. The only remaining question is whether the wings come off before or after impact with the ground. The sunlit landscape of Cowichan Bay whipped around, ZLG stood on its ear, and the g loading dragged my cheeks into bulldog jowls before Doug returned us to normal flight. I laughed nervously as I pushed my eyeballs back into place.

For the next lesson with Derek, stalls, slow flight, and spins were on the menu—the slow, uncomfortable, end of the flight envelope. An aerodynamic stall has nothing to do with the engine stopping. Driving along the highway one day, hold your hand out of the window, palm downward, fingers together and pointing toward the side of the road. The wind will push your hand backward, but if you tilt it slightly so that the thumb (leading edge) is higher than the trailing edge of your hand, it will produce lift upward. Your hand is an airfoil or wing section; the tilt angle is called "angle of attack." As you increase the angle, the lift increases but so does the drag of the wind pushing your hand backward. Beyond a certain angle there is an abrupt loss of lift and increase in drag. You will feel a tickling sensation on the back of your hand as the airflow breaks away from it, and this breaking away of the airflow is one reason why it will not produce lift any more. That angle is the stalling angle of attack—your hand stalled. Any airfoil, be it a wing, a fan blade, a sail, or a boat's rudder, has a stalling angle of attack.

You also may feel unpredictable flip-flop forces trying to alter the tilt angle of your hand. Unless it is anchored like a fan blade, or controlled as by an aircraft's tail, an airfoil is inherently unstable, which is why "flying wing" aircraft have never really succeeded and many of them have crashed.

But what happens when an aircraft stalls? The nose pitches downward out of the pilot's control, and the aircraft begins to fall. But does it keep on falling? No sir. The pilot releases the pressure on the controls which brought the wings to the stalling angle of attack in the first place, unstalls the wings, and flies on, unless he stalled the aircraft close to the ground, in which case other unpleasant things may happen. There is also a partly stalled condition called "mushing," when the wings are not producing enough lift for the pilot's needs at the time. Hard landings more often result from mushing than from outright stalling. The stalling characteristics are intrinsic to the design of both the wing itself and the aircraft as a whole. A Cessna 152 stalls reluctantly and gently, and unstalls happily. One of Doug's sayings was, "The aircraft wants to fly, but some of these dumb pilots won't let it." Of course, that is not the whole story on stalls, but it will do for now.

"And show me a stall. Carb heat hot, power off, back on the yoke, back, back, keep it straight with the rudder, don't use the ailerons, right back with the yoke." By now the aircraft has its nose in the air, swinging slightly from side to side. The stall warning is letting out a continuous and sinister whine. Whoof! The nose drops all of a sudden; the ground comes up and looks at us. "And recover." Release the back pressure on the yoke that stalled it in the first place and we are sitting on hard, solid air with the wind hissing in our wings.

The wonder of the air's solidity was lost on me, and flying became a battle with an irrational fear. Stalls might have shown my frozen brain that the aircraft floats in the sky; it bounces on the air; the solid ground is merely a convenient reference plane indicating the direction of that force field called gravity.

An aircraft is the only device used by normal mortals which transports them into a medium rather than along the interface between media. We live on the ground—the earth-air interface. Sometimes we go out in boats—on the water-air interface. Some of us penetrate the earth medium in mines or tunnels. Even fewer of us go down into the water medium in submarines or as divers. But we are creatures of the interface, and when we launch ourselves away from it, we can survive only by means of elaborate life-support and guidance systems, and in many cases we are terrified. Take away our familiar reference planes and the secure knowledge of which way is up, and we are lost.

An aircraft will fly at a variety of speeds. The wing produces lift because of its motion through the air and because of its angle of attack. At high speed the angle of attack needed for the wing to produce enough lift to sustain the airplane in flight is quite small. At lower speeds, however, the angle of attack must be increased if the aircraft is to maintain level flight. In the end a speed is reached which is so slow that the necessary angle of attack comes to equal the stalling angle of attack of the particular wing. That speed is called the stalling speed, although the aircraft can stall at any other speed if the wing is brought to the stalling angle of attack—which the pilot can do, intentionally or otherwise, by means of the elevators, which are controlled by the yoke or stick.

Below normal cruising speed, below best glide speed, and down as far as the so-called stalling speed is a regime of flying slowly at high angles of attack called "slow flight." In slow flight the wing is near its stalling angle of attack and can be stalled inadvertently. Because of the aircraft's low speed, the authority of the control surfaces is reduced, and the aircraft differs in other respects from its behavior at normal flying speeds. For these and other reasons slow flight requires careful handling and is a necessary part of flight training. I understood little or nothing of this at the time, but I went through the motions and chased the numbers as instructed.

In a stall the aircraft may want to yaw and, if the pilot does not check this tendency, a spin results. On this occasion we were flying IMH, a blue and white Cessna 152 with slinky drooped wingtips—to which I attributed sinister intent on Derek's part. Derek warned me that he was about to demonstrate a spin, even to the extent of remarking that the aircraft might turn upside down. I sat back thinking nothing of it. I had seen the SE-5 spin at the Farnborough Airshow in 1960. Nothing to it. The event hit me like a bombshell. All the senses work overtime; collectively they are appalled. The eyes see that the ground has appeared where the sky used to be and is doing several things that it should not. The innards are filled with alarm at the sensation of utterly falling and tumbling at once. The ears take in the stall warning, whining, crescendo, like an angry cat, the creaking of the aircraft, and the swooshing of wind in its stalled wings. The abnormal airflow around the engine wafts its warm smell into the cockpit. The combined assault on the senses is terrifying.

Derek asked in a concerned voice: "Were you scared?" I replied, "Not particularly," but only because I think slowly and had not had time to get into a fully developed funk. Anyone who was not scared by his first spin was either stupid, a liar, or had his eyes shut at the time.

Spins lurked like a black shadow at the edge of the flight envelope. We didn't do any more before Derek started to teach me how to return the aircraft to earth in usable condition. But it was clear that a pilot had to be totally insensitive to stall a 152 inadvertently, and that it would not spin unless stalled first. I was satisfied that I could avoid stalls, spins, and spiral dives, and that sufficed for the present.

Because I had alternated between Doug and Derek as instructors, neither was quite willing to entrust me with the takeoff until lesson 4 or 5. Aircraft are reluctant to stay on the runway centerline once airborne. They yaw, they drift, they slide sideways, or all three. The novice must therefore learn to control these wayward tendencies. I had finally inspired enough confidence in Derek for him to allow me to fly ZLG off the ground. We had just taken off when I noticed that we were drifting toward the grass beside the runway. It was then that I realized we were flying. It was no longer relevant what the wheels were running on because they were not running on anything except fresh air.

We bounced and jolted in the turbulence over the hills of Saltspring Island. Derek put me through my paces on medium and steep turns. To my frustration and disgust I made a complete hash of them. "Recovery from unusual attitudes" was also on the agenda. Derek put the aircraft into some mildly abnormal postures, and it was correspondingly simple to return to normal flight. We used power line cuts and straight sections of roads to simulate the landing pattern around a runway, which was the next stage in the game.

On our return the control tower cleared us to a straight-in approach to runway 08 over the water of the Saanich Inlet. Without Derek's prompting I would have flown straight on over the runway at the traffic circuit height of 800 feet. There is a natural tendency in flight to feel that things are fine as they are, and it takes conscious effort to maneuver the aircraft closer to the ground.

Contrary to most people's beliefs, an aircraft is reluctant to go down. As it descends, it tends to pick up speed; the faster it goes, the more it wants to fly. If it arrives at the runway threshold too fast, it will disdain the ground and nothing will induce it to land. Plenty of people have piled into the obstructions at the far ends of runways as a result. If, on the other hand, the aircraft is too slow on final approach, it does not fly well and is vulnerable to wind gusts. Too low as well, and it is fixing to flop down amongst the approach lights. Therefore, the approach to land is the first maneuver in which the pupil must fly at a more or less exact airspeed. Admittedly in a Cessna 152 anything from 55 to 65 knots will produce the desired result, but the margins are definitely set.

But what was this? Here was my seventh flying lesson, totaling nearly seven hours of dual instruction, and we had not even progressed as far as landings. Everyone in the how-to-fly books went solo after seven or eight hours. The hot rocks soloed before that. It was obvious that I was not going to solo in eight hours and was not a hot rock either. To look facts in the face, I was a nervous, awkward sprog pilot—and not even a good one.

6

Circuits and Thuds

Any flight has to end in a landing of some sort, preferably one which minimizes wear and tear on the aircraft and its occupants and avoids damaging the scenery. The idea is to persuade the aircraft to quit flying at a narrowly specified time and place. It goes without saying that the pupil must be able to do this before he can be sent flying on his own. It is a delicate maneuver, hard to learn, hard to teach, hard to analyze, hard to do well. Millions of words have been written about it. More people bend more airplanes (and worse) by doing it wrong than by any other means. Many people must have wondered if it would not be easier to switch everything off and land the aircraft with a big parachute. Some people, generally between the ages of sixteen and twenty, take to it like ducks to water. Some people never learn—and never solo. It took me a month, and eleven hours of dual instruction, to learn a phase of flight lasting less than two minutes.

So what happens? The real business of landing a small plane begins 400 feet above ground and 4,000 feet back from the beginning of the runway, at the turn onto final approach. From there the airplane descends gently with a little power, slightly nose-down, fast enough to fly smoothly but not much faster. This path carries it to a point just beyond the runway threshold and about 20 feet above the center of the runway. At that point the pilot starts to break the descent or "flare out" (nothing to do with pyrotechnics!). After the flare the aircraft is slightly nose-up, with its wheels a few inches above the runway, ready to land like a duck. It "floats" briefly for 300–500 feet along the runway as the wings give up their lift, and then settles gently onto the ground. A light aircraft will then roll to a stop with little or no use of brakes.

The pilot's task is to translate what he sees, hears, and feels into control pressures and movements of throttle, trim, and flaps which will make the airplane do what it is supposed to do. He must compress his vision from the broad vista of the sky to a slab of black asphalt. Having spent his flight staying well away from the ground, he must now tuck himself into it. He controls the aircraft by looking ahead over the nose, yet he must judge the height of his unseen wheels above the ground to a matter of inches. For the pupil both the sensory cues and the knowledge of what to do about them are still quite unfamiliar.

Wind does little to make things easier. When the aircraft is flying, it moves with the air like a fish in a river. When it is on the ground, it is a lifeless object and the wind blows over it. When it is betwixt and between, let the pilot beware! A headwind will steepen the approach flight; a tailwind will waft the aircraft farther along the runway. A crosswind will drift it off the runway centerline; the consequences of landing with the aircraft drifting sideways range from discomfort to disaster. Moving air clings to the ground so that wind blowing up or down slopes near the runway will cause the aircraft to rise or sink. Buildings and trees near the touchdown area may stream turbulent wakes across the pilot's path, as do other aircraft. Wind may change both strength and direction with increasing height above the ground, with or without layers of turbulent wind shear in between. A fast, heavy aircraft such as an airliner will plow through many of the lesser motions of the air, but the light plane pilot soon learns about every quirk of the wind near the ground.

To learn to land, you must first take off. Come with me—let's fly around the patch. You are in the hot seat. The tower has cleared you for takeoff. You taxi out to the middle of the runway and line up on the centerline. Gently your right hand pushes the throttle all the way forward, your right foot squeezing a little pressure onto the rudder pedal, for the bellowing engine wants to swing the aircraft left. The fingers of your left hand feel the yoke start to come alive and, with a light backward pressure, you run the nosewheel lightly along the ground. The airspeed indicator wakes up, and soon the aircraft lifts off. With gentle yoke pressures you hold the airspeed around 65–70 knots and keep the wings level, but the nose is pointing left of the runway, the runway itself appears below your left elbow, and you are not sure how it got there.

The altimeter tells you that there is 400 feet of nothing under you. You dip the nose to look for airplanes ahead and climb to 500 feet, where you start a climbing left turn. Your instructor reminds you quite sharply not to let the bank steepen beyond 15°. You stop the bank from increasing with gentle but persistent aileron and rudder pressures. Perhaps he remembers too vividly someone who stalled out of the initial climbing turn, spun, crashed, and burned right in the middle of the airfield.

You straighten out more or less at right angles to the runway. You reach circuit height and must level out and turn left at the same time. In making the turn, you leave too much power on and the aircraft has climbed another hundred feet or even two before you notice. Your instructor points this out to you and also remarks that you are wandering away from the airport at a distressing rate. You correct both of these, whereupon he asks, "What should you be doing now?" No intelligent response detected.

The pre-landing check! Fuel-on-both-and-sufficient-mixture-rich-carb-heat-hot-oil-temperature-and-pressure-check-brakes-check. What else? Call the tower on the radio, getting your call in edgeways between the radio chatter: "Zulu Lima Golf downwind left on two-six." The loudspeaker in the cabin roof pukes all over you: "Zulu-Lima-Golf-number-three-to-land-number-two-on-twenty-six-look-out-for-a-King-Air-directly-beneath-you-final-on-thirty-one-your-traffic-is-a-Bandeirante-on-a-wide-left-base." You hold the microphone in your hand, wondering what on earth to say. Meanwhile the aircraft has lost a hundred feet and is trying to sneak away from the airport again. Your instructor takes the microphone, talks to the tower, and asks if you see the "traffic," which you don't. Seeing other aircraft in flight is an acquired skill.

The flow of information into your ears would baffle a computer. The airplane talks to you with engine and slipstream noise. Your instructor warms your starboard ear. The radio loudspeaker warms both ears, and you have to pick out of the babble the bits that are for you. You do not have much time to sort it out.

The airfield is laid out at your left elbow. You are flying parallel to the active runway, but in the opposite direction to which you will eventually land. As the threshold passes 45° behind your left shoulder, you ease back on the throttle and make a descending left turn, holding the nose up and working the trim wheel to bring the airspeed back to 70 knots. You can't see the runway because the wing is in the way as you bank toward it. You should have picked an aiming mark off your left wingtip before you started the turn, but you forgot. You lift the wing to have a look, and go on with the turn. Your instructor wonders out loud why you can't make the turn in one smooth coordinated movement. You straighten out on base leg and put the flap switch to 10°.

The runway comes abeam of you and you turn in toward it. You can't seem to get it right and either overshoot or undershoot the turn. The turn onto final approach is another maneuver in which people sometimes dump themselves onto the ground, so you are quite cautious about it.

Your instructor is coaching you all the way down final approach because this is the main purpose of everything you have done since you took off.

You jockey the aircraft with little adjustments to the throttle and little slips and skids. You are tense. The black runway ahead grows at you. The threshold with the white numbers "26" slides beneath you. Now you are down over the runway itself: You need no prompting to raise the nose because the hard, black asphalt with the blacker screech marks of aircraft tires is coming up toward you. It obsesses you. You peer at it over the nose. It rushes by beneath you. Keep the aircraft straight with the rudder or the pesky thing will fly sideways. You hold the yoke in an iron grasp and pull it slowly back toward you. The aircraft decides that it has had enough; you feel it dropping out from under you and, sure enough, the hard, hard runway is waiting to receive you...bamscreech! Sorry, airplane; sorry, instructor; sorry, runway; sorry, Transport Canada.

And you take off again for another try. Six of these excursions will fill an hour's tuition.

Even in still air with no disturbances, it is not easy to learn these maneuvers. The showery skies of April and early May were not the easiest place for me to learn. Thick cloud decks concealed embedded cumulonimbus cells, which showed up only as areas of heavier rain but which let out downdrafts and turbulent gusty winds. There was a resident downdraft over the threshold of runway 26. I wondered if the Flying Club had the means to turn it on and off. The tower put in its ten cents' worth with instructions to "widen it out," "tighten it up," "extend your downwind," "square your base leg," "overshoot from your present position," and generally get out of the way of the complex, high-performance aircraft and their invisible but lethal wake vortices.

Derek and I blasted off in ZLG one Sunday afternoon to practice some maneuvers near Duncan before returning to the circuit. I made a right turn after takeoff that put us neatly over Deep Cove. We got there just as a cloud of airplanes converged on it and whizzed by us, seen and unseen, so this was none too popular with Derek. I did not realize at the time that Deep Cove was the reporting point for all inbound VFR traffic from the northwest. Besides, I had enough of a job controlling the aircraft and preventing it from hurling itself to the ground. All ground-pounders know that aircraft have this tendency and only the most extreme skill and vigilance on the part of the pilot will prevent them from doing so. One day the acolyte begins to realize that this is not so and starts to unfreeze his brain, navigate, talk to people on the radio, admire the view, and generally have a good time.

We flew about over Duncan before rejoining the circuit. It was time for me to try my profusely sweating hand at an actual landing. My mouth felt as if it were lined with shotcrete. My first attempt dropped us hard onto the runway. Effort number 2, by a fluke, was remarkably smooth. Effort number 3 banged in as before.

The next lesson was on a dark, showery evening. With daylight-saving time in effect, there was more time for flying in the evenings when weather and traffic conditions tended to be quieter. This time the wind shifted so fast that we used three different runways for three consecutive touch-and-go landings. Everything went surprisingly well. Derek introduced me to landing with the flaps extended 30° instead of 10° as hitherto. Cessnas have flaps like hangar doors. With full flaps and power off, the aircraft seemed to point straight at the ground, hanging on its flaps as if on a parachute.

The how-to-fly books never said anything about wind, or not much. First you learned to fly in a headwind, then you graduated to crosswind landings. Obviously the authors lived in some part of the world where these things could be arranged to order. They did not seem to go in for approaches through turbulence, wind shear, and downdrafts. For me every landing seemed to be crosswind, even when there was no wind to speak of. The aircraft kept slipping mischievously to the right.

Emergencies! Fire, engine failure, radio failure, engine failure on takeoff! After Derek's briefing on these unpleasant possibilities, I was much tempted to stay on the ground. Once we were in the air, Derek would whisper into the microphone in furtive colloquy with the tower and then declare some ghastly emergency requiring an immediate power-off forced landing. Carb heat hot, glide toward the nearest runway. Too high, too close, don't dive at the runway, don't know what to do, that's what flaps are for stupid, full flaps, make like a Stuka, better flare out, not yet we're still 50 feet in the air, there's the gas truck beside the runway, flare out again lower down, in my next incarnation I want to be an airport gas truck driver, another swoop, don't stall it, plunk-screech, carb heat cold, flaps up, full power, snap glance to make sure the flaps are retracting, wonder if we'll have enough runway (Derek would say if not), and we're skittering in a crosswind and airborne once more, climbing crabwise over the runway.

One day Derek was going to climb out and say, "Take it round by yourself." I had a notion that that day was not far off, and it began to obsess me. My thirteenth flying lesson was on Friday the Thirteenth, and I did not want to go solo. In fact, it was a gray, blustery evening, and I did not even want to fly. My toes were putting roots into the wet asphalt. Mentally I tugged at Derek's sleeve: "Look at that black cloud. It's going to eat us and spit out the pieces." As we walked out to the aircraft, Martin Tucker remarked pointedly, "It's been nice knowing you guys." Martin looked after the airplanes. Now he's an airline pilot. Nice guy!

We strapped ourselves into ZLG's flimsy structure, while it rocked and creaked in the wind which whistled around it. What am I doing here, and why? I must be crazy. But at least I have the common sense to be nervous. This other guy, he's not even nervous.

There was so much wind that we forsook the everlasting grind around the circuit for the upper air. The best piece of upper air was over the islands. Sunbeams broke through the cloud ceiling close overhead and drew their wandering fingers across islands on a steel-gray sea. To the west the mountains of Vancouver Island merged with the slate-gray mass of the storm. Derek had a habit of pulling rabbits out of the hat, and in truth I was becoming spooked. I was scared stiff that he was going to haul off into a ghastly spin, and I was somewhat relieved when we turned for home.

Another dark, windy May evening, and my efforts at landing grew worse and worse. I banged the airplane onto the ground, landed while it was drifting sideways, and so it went on. My ideas of going solo disintegrated. I knew that if I were alone in the aircraft at that instant, I would smash it and myself trying to get it onto the ground. We were both tense with frustration. In the end Derek took control and we called it quits. One of the people around the Flying Club asked conversationally when I would be going solo. I looked at him as if he were demented. I went away in utter dejection, but not without having booked the next lesson and having noticed a few things which I intended to try out the next time around.

7

Solo

It was a warm, calm evening when next I went to the Flying Club. Derek had gone. Doug greeted me with a grin and told me that Derek had taken wing for Yellowknife in the Northwest Territories for a flying job there. I had worked in the mines at Yellowknife, so I remarked, "The man's crazy," and left it at that.

I explained my problem to Doug and what I proposed to do about it. He agreed and added some suggestions of his own as we walked out to the aircraft.

Doug was a peaceful man, secure in himself and monumentally patient. Derek had taught me various types of approaches—power on, power off, full flaps, partial flaps, no flaps—while the basic technique of landing the aircraft still eluded me. Doug dissected what I was doing and took me right back to Square One. I spent more time looking outside and less time looking at the gauges, and flew better as a result. The new landing technique worked well.

Doug told me to look at the far end of the runway, not at the speeding asphalt under the nose. We came dreaming in on final approach, the aircraft neither dawdling nor hurrying. I took in the big picture of the whole runway. As we flared out, I gazed into the distance far off down the runway. When the airplane was good and ready, sure enough it landed with a chirrup from the tires. Doug said that I was waggling the wings too much on final approach, so I took to correcting the aircraft's position with little slips and skids, whereupon life became much easier. My first solo was obviously a part of the distant future, so I relaxed just a little and went away feeling much happier.

A number of small things made a surprising amount of difference. I bought a pair of soft, floppy shoes and flew better. I have worn them for flying ever since. Doug remarked with some surprise, "You're not keeping the wings level." After the lesson I gave it some thought. In a Cessna 152 there is an elbow rest on the door. I had been resting my elbow on it and leaning slightly to the left. Unwittingly I had been flying so that I was upright and the aircraft was minutely banked to the right. Only the airplane noticed. That was why I could never fly straight and why I was always fighting nonexistent crosswinds on landing. I kept my elbow off the rest and everything came out straight. We were getting the bugs corralled into a tight corner. Did I but know it, I would solo in less than a week. One night I dreamed that I flew solo in an aircraft with dark blue stripes. Only IMH had dark blue stripes, whereas we usually flew ZLG, which had red stripes.

We flew a couple of lessons in IMH on warm, still evenings. This was how light plane flying should be, floating through the luminous air of a summer evening. During the next lesson my landings were none too bad. My brain unfroze, and I even understood what the tower was saying on the radio. The wind was picking up as we taxied IMH around to the back of the hangar. It whistled about us, and the aircraft rocked on its wheels. Doug said, "If it hadn't been for this wind, I would have sent you solo." So I nearly went solo in an aircraft with dark blue stripes.

The last evening of May was going to be The Day, unless I was remarkably fumble-fisted or the weather was bad. One of the current sayings was, "Sure I want to go solo, but I don't want to do it alone." What would happen if I got cold feet and chickened out at the last minute? Such things do not bear thinking about. Most people have their own "what-ifs," and 99.999% do not happen. Anyhow the affair had to be got on with.

We took ZLG around the patch a few times. My performance was so grim that I thought, "He'll never send me solo after this," and heaved a secret sigh, although whether of relief or resignation I know not.

We were on final approach, the whole airfield spread out before us. Doug said, "Make this a full stop." We had been flying for only 45 minutes instead of an hour. The moment was at hand. I made a tolerable landing. We taxied in to a slot on the flight line. Doug told me to keep the engine running, unbuckled himself, and climbed out.

On the next slot Brian Truitt and his son, Steve, were preflighting IMH. Steve had soloed a few days before. They both gave me an enthusiastic thumbs-up. Ground control allowed me to go on my way. The business end of runway 08 was a mile from the Flying Club at the end of a long, straight taxiway. A lonely pilot taxied pensively across a vast and, for the time being, deserted airfield. The evening was cool and still with a high overcast—perfect. The airplane and I finally reached the end of the taxiway, which meant that I had to abandon this bucolic pace and launch myself into the air.

I ran the engine up meticulously and fiddled with all the knobs and switches. There was no reason for further delay. This was It. I slewed the aircraft around and looked up the approach path. There was no aviatic life anywhere. The whole of creation had stopped in its tracks to watch me go solo. Even the air was still beneath the bland overcast. The pounding of my heart seemed to shake the aircraft. I drew a deep breath.

"Tower, Zulu Lima Golf ready for takeoff on zero eight."

"Zulu Lima Golf cleared for takeoff."

Derek had always made me track the yellow line which curved out onto the runway. I had never been able to feel that following yellow lines was the apogee of the aviator's art, and I gleefully ignored it. I lined up on the center of the runway and gently applied full throttle. ZLG finally wearied of the ground and floated into the sky. I felt enormous exhilaration and relief—exhilaration because I was at last flying an aircraft by myself, relief because it was suddenly, for the moment, so easy. It was a piece of cake. It was refreshing to be alone. There was so much elbow room, and I could see in all directions. (Doug was not a small man.)

I found myself on the downwind leg of the circuit at 800 feet, reported to the tower, flew on for a while, cut back on the power, turned onto base leg, brought the airspeed back to 70 knots, extended 10° of flap, and turned onto final approach. My intense concentration did not prevent me from noticing a small blue and white aircraft sitting beside the runway. The landing went as smoothly as the rest of the flight, with a faint chirrup from the wheels. A voice floated over the radio: "Nice one, Tom." I jumped and wandered all over the runway, waving my ailerons in true lesson #1 style. The tower controller went wild: "Who said that? Who said that?" I wondered the same thing myself. It was Brian Truitt, who had been waiting to take off.

I taxied in, shut everything down, and secured the aircraft with the utmost deliberation. I whispered, "Thanks, airplane," and marched back to the clubhouse unable to suppress a grin from ear to ear. Doug feigned surprise. His eyebrows shot up.

"Ah! Back already? How did it go?"

"Nice. Easy. Fickle things, airplanes, Doug. It flew without you."

There was no one else about. Doug gave me the Flying Club's solo certificate. I offered him a bottle of pop from the machine, which was the only available means of celebration, but he did not seem to drink pop. He accepted my profuse thanks for his patience. I walked away on air. I had flown solo.

Transport Canada says in its *Flight Training Manual:* "The first solo is a landmark in your flying career. . . . The amount of dual instruction required to solo need not be a reflection of your ability. Everyone varies in their capacity to learn, and very often the pupil who is a little slow to learn ultimately makes the better pilot." Comforting words. The number of hours of dual instruction needed to reach first solo is not supposed to matter, but not many pilots have forgotten how many hours it took them to solo, and how that compared with the average at the time and place where they did so.

In the military, they wash you out if you do not solo fast enough, because they are not going to spend a million gallons of jet fuel teaching you to fly.

There was the fellow who had learned to fly at the Victoria Flying Club thirty years ago: "I was scared stiff on my first solo. They spent three hours scaring the daylights out of you, one hour teaching you to fly, then they sent you solo."

One member of our groundschool class went solo after ten hours. We crowded round and asked what it had been like. He said it had frightened him. We all looked at each other. Another character soloed after ten hours, but on a subsequent takeoff he got his feet mixed up, reinforcing the aircraft's tendency to turn left instead of counteracting it. He aborted the takeoff before reaching the grass at the edge of the runway but frightened himself so badly that he didn't fly for another month, and not much after that.

I went solo after nineteen hours and found it as easy as falling off a log. My boss had taken twenty-two hours of, albeit discontinuous, tuition before going solo. Brian Truitt was heard to remark: "What's Tom worrying about? It took me twenty-five hours." My friend Harvey Taggart chalked up twenty-seven hours before flying solo in a Cessna 172 and, even so, found it something of a strain. Some of our aviatrices completed over thirty hours before they went solo, or gave up flying, or both in succession. What they lacked in aptitude they made up for in sheer determination.

Perhaps it can be truthfully said that if a civilian student pilot has not come within spitting distance of flying solo after twenty hours of dual instruction, it is time for a serious appraisal of the problem. Something like $1,500 will have gone west in tuition fees and other expenses—with much more to follow—and the signer of the checks should consider seriously if further expenditure is justified.

Whatever they say, however long it takes to get there, and whatever trials and tribulations may follow, the first solo is a Big Deal and nothing can detract from the triumph of its achievement.

8

Back to School

While some fifteen or twenty people were going through various stages of their airborne antics in the blue and not so blue skies around Victoria, a similar number of us attended a series of lectures collectively known as groundschool. The Flying Club ran three private pilot groundschools each year, as well as groundschools for commercial and instrument training, so the upstairs classrooms were a hive of industry for several evenings each week.

This particular groundschool class convened on April 11 at seven o'clock, and seventeen 3-hour sessions followed on Mondays and Wednesdays until June 8. The subjects covered were:

- The voluminous and occasionally baffling contents of a publication called *A.I.P.Canada (Aeronautical Information Publication Canada)*—a subject known generically as "Air Regulations"
- The structure and components of aircraft
- Aero engines, their ancillary systems, and how to look after them
- Theory of flight, why and how airplanes fly, and why they sometimes refuse to do so at awkward moments
- The magic numbers of aircraft performance and the importance of weight and balance
- Navigation, or how to get there from here without getting lost or running out of gas
- Meteorology, and especially how to read the streams of numbers and codewords that make up the aviation weather reports.

These are necessary aspects of learning to fly, indeed of surviving when off the ground, and can best be taught in a classroom. After the end of the groundschool course came the private pilot written examination.

It was quite a scramble to get home from work, bathe, change clothes, eat, and head out to the airport. Perhaps not all of us were equally wide awake. The instructors must have thought we had solid clay between the ears. If they asked a question, half the class did not want to look too foolish, and the other half did not want to look too smart. At first we eyed each other suspiciously, but groundschool soon became our rap session.

The civilian student pilot often battles on in lonely limbo. The relationship with the instructor is an impersonal one despite an interdependence bordering on symbiosis and close physical proximity in a cockleshell craft of the skies. The question, "How am I doing?" will seldom draw a forthright answer. Praise might be inappropriate because perhaps nothing praiseworthy had occurred. On the other hand, a searing analysis of the pupil's more ghastly mistakes during the past hour of cosurvival might rob the instructor of his trade. Attempts to draw out the instructor's own experiences as a pupil may encounter little success. Many pupils have no one versed in the technicalities of flight in whom to confide. There is a longing, deep down inside, to say: "Tell me that I am not alone. Tell me that others suffer the same fears and failures and frustrations as I do. Tell me that others make the same blunders." That is one reason why this book is written.

From a more materialistic standpoint the civilian student pilot sees himself spending money like water on something which is, to a greater or lesser extent, both frightening and unnecessary. No sensible person can escape serious misgivings.

At groundschool we shared our fears and failures and our joys. We found that if someone had trouble with one thing, someone else had worse trouble with another. One had trouble with flying; one had trouble with groundschool; another suffered from airsickness. We all had battles with the medics who strove to cancel our aspirations on pretexts ranging from myopia to flatulence. When some of our number went solo, we were happy with them and lined up to congratulate them and ask what it was like. Some of us gave up flying but, curiously enough, they did so after the end of the groundschool course. The end of the rap sessions and the loss of mutual support played their part.

At the start of the first session, I was the first to arrive, apart from a huge individual with a briefcase and a stack of books. I introduced myself by name. He introduced himself as Harvey Taggart. He lived on my route to the airport, so we car-pooled to groundschool. We were at the same stage in learning to fly, and having similar problems. We laughed at the same things and became firm friends.

But at times that ease of flight, which we so earnestly desired, seemed so terribly far away, the sky so unattainable and, if attained, so filled with crushing demands that we could so inadequately meet.

There was, for instance, the case of time warp. We had just reached the airport one fine evening on the way to groundschool. Then we saw them: two Voodoos in tight formation, coming at us at a hundred feet, rustling past the control tower, squat, black, and deadly against the evening sky.

Take a microsecond, an infinitesimal fragment of time. Shave flakes off it so fine that they curl at the edges. Two long, gray bullets, their noses lifting, solid black thunder tearing the earth with glass-hard claws, shock diamonds of pure orange flame exploding from their afterburners. For that flake of time they are there, and they are gone, rolling and rolling and rolling, falling ever upward into the blue firmament until nothing remains but a pencil line of sound drawn across the bass drum of the sky.

The airfield slowly comes alive, antediluvian in its slowness, decrepit, thistles growing in cracked concrete, little prehistoric airplanes with faded paint. The 727 that started its takeoff roll several hours ago lumbers reluctantly into the air, past the gas truck sleeping amongst the weeds. That Cessna on final approach, the pilot hung it on a piece of sky. Put his feet on the instrument panel and went to sleep. Now the tower is going crazy trying to get him to move it out of the way.

The gyroscopes of time run gradually up to speed. The 727 is climbing away on the evening run to Edmonton. The gas truck is tearing along a taxiway to serve a customer. The Cessna comes dropping down the approach path to a feather-light landing at the far side of the airfield.

Our eyes are blinded once more to the cracked concrete and faded paint. The little airplanes are our friends, and we know them by name. A Cessna 152 is a Very Serious Airplane and V_x is 54 knots and don't forget it. The vision we have seen is etched on our minds. But were they really there? Were *what* really there? Oh, never mind, we'd better get along to groundschool. And gravity dragged at each cell in our bodies separately, because we were ground-pounders.

9

Around the Patch

Once the struggle to achieve solo flight is won, the feeling is of anticlimax. This feeling may, indeed, be such that the soloist never flies again. The natural question is: "What next?" The private pilot flight test is still many months away, and the onward path is not necessarily smooth. Solo flights alternate with further dual instruction. The student is sent off by himself to practice specified maneuvers. The regulations call for a certain number of hours of dual and solo flight to qualify for the flight test, but the student pilot has much to practice, and "building time" (accumulating flight time) is not a problem as it is in the more advanced stages of training.

Before solo flight all effort is devoted to one objective: to take hold of that aircraft, induce it to fly, control it in flight, and then flump it onto the runway again. After solo the development of skills branches out into a skein of parallel paths. The basic maneuvers must become more accurate until they are up to the standards required for the flight test. The fledgling is launched on his first solo in ideal and, above all, quiet conditions. As his skills develop, he is allowed to venture into more demanding conditions of wind and traffic and is left progressively to size up things for himself.

Each aircraft type has a Book of Words describing its systems and performance. For a Cessna 152 the book goes on for 200 pages. One of the items concerns the shortest achievable takeoff and landing distances and the correct methods of obtaining them. There are techniques for operating off short or rough airstrips. The pupil must learn these. He must learn to assess a flat piece of ground as a potential landing ground and align the aircraft so as to be able to carry out a landing. He must learn how to carry out a forced landing should the engine fail. When all these matters are reasonably under way, the matter of pilot navigation raises its head.

A few evenings after soloing, I took off for my first all-solo flight—circuits and landings. Brian Truitt was teaching Harvey Taggart in a Cessna 172, and together we ground our way around the patch.

A week later Doug took me for a lesson on a gray, blustery evening with a strong crosswind. I flew so badly that I thought aloud that Doug must have doubted the wisdom of sending me solo. He smiled serenely and replied that he never entertained such doubts. After that I made no flights for three weeks, first to attend a tunneling convention in Chicago, then to hit the books for the private pilot written exam. After such a gap I needed some more dual, and I soloed all over again to convince myself that I could still fly. I wondered if I would ever escape from the vicinity of the airfield.

Eventually we did. Up in the quiet evening sky we explored the dubious realms of slow flight and stalls. Doug told me to stall ZLG out of a climbing right turn. It takes some horsing around to make a 152 stall, and sometimes it follows its innate tendencies and refuses to do so. ZLG slumped back into level flight.

"And now show me a stall out of a climbing *left* turn." That produced results in no uncertain fashion. Wham! The aircraft suddenly turned upside down, the controls lifeless in my hand. I looked up in terror at green fields and the tops of trees gyrating overhead. Somehow the aircraft regained normal flight. With the smile of the satisfied artist, Doug remarked casually: "And there's your incipient spin." We followed through with some steep turns and practiced approaches, then headed for home.

"OK," said Doug, "Now you're cleared to go out to the practice area and have some fun."

Fun?! You battle with your fears. You take an airplane and practice maneuvers until you are giddy and blue in the face. Then you come back to the circuit which is full of multi-thousand-hour pilots in complex high-performance aircraft and thump-screech your little airplane onto the ground. Then you write a check for all this money, and this is fun?

Learning to fly had become a grim struggle. I was not afraid of the aircraft as such, but I was afraid of flight or, more accurately, of being about to fall. Deep down I did not believe in flight. I manipulated the controls as taught, and the earth's familiar perspectives unraveled in strange and beautiful ways, like a child's kaleidoscope, only more so. But this was accompanied by peculiar, and not altogether pleasant, sensations. Inwardly I believed that I was suspended on a string which might break. I knew that my mastery of flight was still tenuous, but I had never done anything seriously wrong, never frightened an instructor, never yelled "You have control!" in the approved manner while airborne.

The hours of successful flight unrolled behind me like a vapor trail, yet I suffered chronically from a lack of self-confidence. How I envied those people who sauntered nonchalantly out to the aircraft, climbed in, and flew away, while I wrestled with my fears and churning insides, and agonized over each chip and scratch in the paint. How do you get *there* from *here*?

Times without number, as I cruised over the Cowichan Valley in the quiet evening sky, the question asked itself: "Why are you doing this?" There were no fewer than six answers.

1. Other people can do it; so can I.
2. It is interesting to be able to look down on things at will.
3. I am hooked on the sheer beauty of the world as seen from a small airplane.
4. Airplanes fascinate me—always have.
5. I am too stubborn to give up.
6. I cannot understand how I survived a life of such utter boredom as the one I must have lived before I began to fly.

Martin Tucker often came and talked to me as I preflighted the airplane on a warm summer evening. He was nineteen, had won his private license the year before, and was working on his commercial. He worked long hours at the Flying Club, looking after the aircraft and keeping the place tidy. I imagined that he had taken to flight as if born in a cockpit (a difficult operation). We stood on the flight line admiring the slate-gray hills silhouetted against the evening sky.

"Terrifying," said Martin.

"What's terrifying?"

"Learning to fly these heavier-than-air machines," was the abstracted reply. So it was not just me.

Doug took me for a lesson in IMH. We were flying over the practice area half a mile behind another 152. Doug said, "Do you want to see an aircraft go into a spin?" I replied that I would be keenly interested provided it was not from inside the aircraft. The other airplane promptly capsized into a spin. The mystery was how Doug could look at another aircraft and see that it was about to spin.

More and more I benefited from the depth of Doug's experience. A reticent man, he would, if pressed, admit to having flown piston-engined fighters and the early jets. At different times he had been an airline pilot and a bush pilot and had taught many hundreds of military and civilian pupils. What Doug did not know about flying was not worth knowing. I flew by the Gospel According to MacColl. His watchword was, "If you are kind and gentle to airplanes, they will be kind and gentle to you"—which reflected his personality. Anyone who was unkind to an airplane within Doug's sight or hearing was assured of a lecture the listener was unlikely to forget.

Coaxing a nervous pupil through 15°-banked turns was the professor of physics teaching a child that water boils at 212°F. But Doug came into his own in teaching the new pilot how to look after himself. The fledgling learned that when the wind ruffled his wings in a certain way, it meant certain things in terms of all the flight that ever was and all the weather systems that ever were, and he was to react accordingly.

Doug was absolutely attuned to the forces of nature, and he had a profound knowledge of the insides of airplanes. I often hung around just listening as he expounded on something to another of his pupils. Harvey Taggart told me, wide-eyed, of the time when they noticed a boat aground. Doug remarked: "He'll be off in a while; the tide's coming in." Said Harvey: "The man is teaching me to fly. We are interested in wind and clouds and airplanes, and he even knows the state of the tide." Doug could not only teach one pupil circuits and landings, but he could also watch other pilots in the circuit and assess their performance.

One evening there were thunderstorms over the hills but none near the airfield. Golden jags of lightning burst from clouds of the richest purple-gray. Doug remarked, "I don't mind thunderstorms as long as I can see them."

"Have you ever been caught in a thunderstorm?" I asked.

"No," he replied pensively, "I generally avoid them."

The light plane pilot is a mouse. Weather, mountains, mechanical failure, and limitations of skill are, collectively, the cat. Some mice will look out of their holes and see the cat. They may think the cat is asleep, it does not eat mice, they can cross the floor too fast for it to catch them, or it is a stuffed cat. They reach the middle of the floor before discovering that they were wrong on all counts. Doug would wait until the cat had gone, which accounted for the longevity of the mouse. "Thunderstorms?" said he. "I generally avoid them."

An essential part of the light plane pilot's stock in trade is to be able to land in a field. The student pilot becomes familiar with maneuvering toward a paved rectangular runway with a windsock but must learn to size up any clear surface as a potential landing ground, judge the strength and direction of the wind, and align the aircraft for landing. Landing in fields was by no means an approved procedure and was for emergencies only.

All that glistens is not gold; all airfields are not necessarily good places to land. Duncan airport was a short gravel strip on a hilltop between trees. If the wind blew across the runway, the pilot had to descend through the turbulence off the treetops, through a wind shear, and into the calmer air below. If the wind blew along the runway, the ground sloping down from the threshold drew the air with it, causing a dangerous downward flow of air. It was a notorious trap, and many aircraft had been wrecked there. I swore to avoid it.

Engine failures seldom happen, and more rarely to the proficient pilot than to others. The pilot must, however, know what to do if the event were to happen. The exercise to practice a forced landing consists of throttling the engine to idle, finding a suitable field, carrying out the necessary checks, and gliding in to the final approach. A couple of hundred feet above the ground, by which time it is clear whether the exercise has succeeded, the practice is broken off and full power applied, whereupon the aircraft climbs away. The difficulty lies in getting the approach to an acceptable landing ground right the first time because there is only one time. If the pilot ends up on final approach too low and too far out, down he goes into the obstructions at the near end. If he is too high and too close on final approach, the aircraft will not land but instead will glide into a different set of obstructions at the far end. Wind adds greatly to this problem of judgment. Even after endless practice I could never guarantee that I could do it right. It took more judgment than I possessed.

The small Cessna aircraft have wing flaps which are large in relation to the total size of the wing. This enables them to fly slowly on the final approach to land and thus to operate into and out of small airfields. The large flaps change the shape of the wing markedly when extended and, hence, the way in which the aircraft flies. Landing with flaps fully extended was another aspect of post-solo training that seemed to take me forever to learn. Some private pilots gave up on the attempt and landed with little or no flap extended at all. This had no real effect on their operations, which were conducted on ample runways.

Some of us soldiered on, however, in search of the grail of perfection, in which we were prodigal of time and effort. It took me 200 hours and a commercial license before I had mastered the subject to my own satisfaction.

We all soon realized that we shared the sky with a variety of other creatures from bugs to Boeings. Any flying creature leaves a swirling wake of disturbed air behind it. The larger the creature, the more violent and persistent the wake. In particular, an aircraft's wingtip streams a vortex which, in the case of a jet airliner, has the strength of a small tornado. Next time you have a window seat in an airliner landing or taking off in wet weather, watch for a pencil-line white vapor trail streaming from its wingtip. That is the core of its wingtip vortex. Such vortices can destroy small aircraft in flight or throw them out of control. Strong vortices can persist for three minutes or so, by which time the aircraft causing them can be 10 miles away.

The jet airliners climbed and descended through light plane altitudes quickly; they were easy to spot; they followed known routes which could be avoided. Because almost any aircraft was larger than a Cessna 152, we had to take care while landing on or taking off from any runway recently vacated by another aircraft. If he flew a steep turn accurately, a pilot could get some solid jolts from his own wake, deriving amusement and satisfaction therefrom.

On fine days the sky over Duncan was thickly populated with small aircraft, necessitating a sharp lookout. Less easy to see were the ultralights. The airport management had put its foot down and said: "Keep them things out of here," so the ultralight pilots betook themselves to grass fields, deserted parking lots, and similar places.

One of our students was with an instructor practicing a forced approach into a field. They found themselves eyeball to eyeball with an ultralight doing the same thing in the opposite direction. Both parties fled the scene pronto.

Birds usually stayed out of our way. We learned, however, to recognize the slow, flapping flight of the eagles. They feared nothing, and we stayed out of their way. One of our Cessna 172s hit a seagull in the airport traffic circuit. The pilot said he had been overtaking it when it sideslipped in front of him. It missed the propeller blades and blew apart all over the nosewheel, causing minor damage. I felt sorry for the birds as they scrambled out of the way of a speeding Cessna. After all, they were there first.

The most common occupants of the sky out on the Pacific coast were the clouds. You want clouds? We had them in all shapes and sizes—big ones, little ones, flat ones, puffy ones, high up, low down, in white, gray, pink, or pastel shades. In the sodden depths of winter, shifting fog banks lay thick upon the coast; streamers of mist wreathed the silence between the dripping trees. Quilted stratocumulus decks blanketed the sky. In spring came wild winds sprouting rough cumulus and sometimes cumulonimbus with virgae of hail drifting from their anvil heads. The wild, bumpy skies only gradually mellowed to the velvet smoothness of high summer. As the earth turned once more to its winter sleep, so the sky became cool and damp. Storm systems rolled in from the Pacific. Clouds lowered and thickened. The creeks in the forests came alive under the pouring rains of winter.

Even the smoothest of clouds are an absolute barrier to the visual pilot. Fly into a cloud and you cannot see which way is up and which way down. Your senses and the motion of the aircraft will fool you in seconds. The only way to fly in cloud is by reference to the aircraft's instruments, an ability that can be achieved only through rigorous training with a qualified instructor. Various people without instrument training have tried on a cloud for size. They lost control of the aircraft immediately. The eerie horror of their last radio transmissions shows how terrible was their end. Clouds and the visual pilot are like gold and the disappointed prospector. They is where he ain't.

A cumulonimbus cloud can affect the winds for many miles around. One more or less fine evening runway 13 was in use. A cumulonimbus cell eyed the airfield malevolently from afar. My attempts at flight had struck a depressing trough in the long grind between solo and flight test. I took off in ZLG for yet another session of circuits and landings. I was flying poorly, and my landings were hard, rough affairs. I was close to despair. A Cessna 152 was said to be easy to fly. Even though I had spent time and money like water on tuition and the most assiduous practice, I was still making these rotten landings. After 45 minutes I gave up and taxied in, ready to tear up my student license and walk away from it all. I climbed out of the aircraft.

Hey, wait a minute! The wind! On my first circuit the tower controller had sent me halfway to Saltspring Island while a Boeing 727 on the runway sorted out some problem or other. In that time the outflow from the cumulonimbus cell had reached the airport. The wind had about-faced, and I had been landing in a 10-knot tailwind. So had all the hotshot commercial pilots in their complex high-performance aircraft. No one had even noticed! I decided to keep my license for a while.

—10

Over the Hills and Far Away

As soon as the first aviators flew far enough to be over unfamiliar territory, navigation became a problem, and has remained so ever since. The freedom to transcend the restrictions of surface routes brought with it the freedom to become lost and the responsibility not to. Although the pilot soon comes to know the lay of the land surrounding his home base as it looks from the air, as soon as he pushes out into more distant territory, he must plan his flight with considerable care. He follows his plotted route, once airborne, by a combination of map reading and a system of bearings and times en route known as "dead reckoning." There are radio beacons on the ground for his benefit if he has the equipment to receive their signals and the understanding to interpret them.

Navigation is an essential part of any private pilot course and, after some navigation training flights with an instructor, the student pilot is sent away on his first solo cross-country flight, an event second only in importance to the first solo flight.

Over much of North America student pilots have an ample terrain over which to exercise their navigation skills. In southwestern British Columbia, however, we were surrounded by geographical barriers which our instructors did not wish us to penetrate at this stage in our training. North and west were the uninhabited mountain ranges of Vancouver Island. South and east were the sea straits which separated Vancouver Island from the mainland. For this reason the Victoria Flying Club's student solo cross-country trip ran up the inhabited coastal plain on the east side of the island for about a hundred miles to a place called Campbell River.

Victoria lies at the southeastern tip of Vancouver Island, about 40 miles from the city and port of Vancouver that stands on the mainland shore on the north side of the Fraser River delta. To the southeast lie Puget Sound and Seattle; to the south the island is separated by the Strait of Juan de Fuca from the Olympic Peninsula of Washington.

Vancouver Island is roughly lozenge-shaped, lying northwest-southeast between 10 and 30 miles off the Canadian mainland. It is some 75 miles wide at most, although such distances mean little because of the indented nature of the west coast which fronts onto the Pacific. The island is almost entirely mountainous, the highest peaks rising to 7,000 feet. Except at their higher elevations the mountains are covered by dense rain forest; countless lakes nestle in hollows and valleys. The greater part of the island, 250 miles long from end to end, is uninhabited, the whole population numbering hardly more than 300,000. Most of these people live in Victoria, and most of the remainder on a narrow coastal plain on the sheltered east side facing the mainland.

The island's settled country extends as far north as Campbell River, with a few isolated settlements farther north and along the west coast. Much of the island is inaccessible other than by boat, floatplane, or helicopter. Any point north of Victoria is known as "up island" (although I have yet to discover if "down island" is equally used in the north). A great multitude of islands of all shapes and sizes dots the straits between Vancouver Island and the mainland.

On the mainland shore the Fraser River floodplain stretches inland as a long triangle for about 50 miles. South lie the mountains of northern Washington. North are the Coast Ranges of British Columbia.

Mountain flying can be hazardous to the uninitiated. For this reason the Victoria Flying Club would not allow a flight into mountain country unless the pilot had been given at least a rudimentary training in the hazards to avoid and the techniques to avoid them. Not least among the hazards is the vicious weather that can develop in the mountains. Therefore, our mountain flying tended to be a summer affair only.

Every summer the Flying Club organized "Mountain Flying Weekends." On the Saturday of the course, Doug MacColl would lecture on the special pitfalls of flying low-powered, light aircraft in the mountains, of which there are many. On the following day four Cessna 172s, each with an instructor and two or three students, would leave on a six-hour flight into the mountainous interior of British Columbia. The students might be more or less experienced private pilots or novices like me. Six hours translates into nearly 600 miles, and we ranged as far afield as Kamloops and the Okanagan Valley.

On this warm, bright Sunday morning in August, Ron McFarlane and I were allocated to Ralph, the Flying Club's newest and hottest instructor. We were to fly to Hope at the entrance to the Fraser Canyon, land, fly on to Penticton in the Okanagan Valley, stop for lunch, return to Hope by a different route, and so fly back to Victoria. I volunteered to fly the first leg to Penticton rather than sit in the back working up a state of nerves. We cobbled a flight plan together, checked our Cessna 172, and waited for Ralph. I had been through navigation in groundschool but had not flown on a cross-country flight.

As I had never flown a Cessna 172, Doug had taken me for a familiarization lesson a few days before. A Cessna 152 has a 110-hp engine, weighs 1,670 lb fully loaded, and seats two. Our Cessna 172s had 160-hp engines, grossed at 2,300 lb, and seated four. The knobs and dials were laid out differently, and the controls felt much heavier.

Ralph finally arrived, looked us up and down, and was not impressed by what he saw. I uncorked it on him that I had flown a 172 for the first time on Friday. His face dropped. It hit the warm asphalt with an audible thud when I told him this was my first cross-country flight. The cogwheels went around in his head: "Why me, man? Why me? Why do I get all the short straws?"

As we enplaned, he said to me, "I'm really going to concentrate on your map-reading." We took off. Having a fistful of 172, I started a normal left turn. Ralph wrenched the aircraft into a right turn, which was the way we were supposed to be going. We wandered up to the colossal height of 7,500 feet and set course for Hope. Ralph started warming my starboard ear about map-reading. Having been an avid map-reader since childhood, I listened obediently and kept my mouth shut.

The blue water shimmered in the sunlight. We could look down sun into its depths marbled by roiling tidal currents. Small boats studded the glassy water in the channels between rocky islands as though suspended in space. A sharp border marked the gray efflux of the Fraser River. To the north lay Vancouver, dimly visible under haze. South were the mountains of northern Washington and Mount Baker's white cone. We flew on over the lower Fraser Valley.

We began our descent near Chilliwack, heading for the entrance to the narrow canyon. The canyon floor was supposed to be 2 miles wide, but it seemed that our wingtips brushed the savage precipices on either side. We floated down to the most perfect surface ever to welcome an airplane's wheels, grass manicured like a lawn. We stretched our legs for fifteen minutes and went our way.

It was a long, growling climb in the heat at full throttle, circling over the town, to reach 7,500 feet. It seemed to take forever before we were again looking down at the mountains and not them at us. Range upon range stretched to the far horizon. We set course up the Coquihalla River and turned east up a barren and forbidding upland valley. Even with 1,500 feet of fresh air beneath us, we wallowed and bumped in the thermals rising from the sun-fried rocks.

We passed over the head of the valley and down a tributary of the Tulameen River. When we reached the Tulameen itself, Ralph said, "Turn right, along this valley." Even I knew that, once over the height of land, we should be flying downstream, regardless of which branch of the Coquihalla we had flown up or which branch of the Tulameen we were flying down. A right turn took us up the valley. Still, the instructor knows best. At least he did until he told me to make a 180° turn and we were on course once more. I began to harbor a suspicion that I had better take a more active part in the proceedings.

We cut across the flat uplands west of Princeton. "That's your valley, straight ahead," declared Ralph, pointing at a V-shaped notch in the hills. When the lay of the land became clearer, I asked, "Are you sure?" Ralph was not quite so sure now. I put in, "That V-shaped valley ahead, that's the Similkameen, right? You can see that cutoff valley running across the spur. Up there to our left are two valleys like the fingers of a hand, a big one and a little one. That's our valley in between."

Quite soon we were flying east by the sun over the only railroad in that part of British Columbia, when Ralph started to worry. Out of the corner of my eye, I watched his fingers stabbing various parts of the map and twiddling the knobs on the VOR set.* He got over it in a while. The railroad gradually disappeared under the fuselage. I turned gently to keep it in sight. Ralph pounced on me: "What are you doing?" "Keeping the iron compass in sight," I replied, which produced the desired silence.

The iron compass duly brought us to the Okanagan Valley over Summerland. We made our descent over the valley and told the

_____

*A VOR is a radio transmitter on the ground, which acts as a navigation beacon. The aircraft's VOR set receives and decodes VOR transmissions.

Penticton tower controller that he was about to have the dubious pleasure of our company. There was no one else about; away from Victoria the sky was empty. Yet here was 6,000 feet of asphalt, a control tower, and all the fixings, just waiting for someone to happen along. I made a rotten landing, and my score promptly went to zero.

Our magic carpet had wafted us from Victoria, including the stop at Hope, in 2 1/2 hours. It would take 8 or 10 hours by car including the ferry trip. To fly there by commercial airliner meant changing planes in Vancouver, so that could not be done in less time. There were so many restrictions on a private license that I was beginning to wonder what the holder *could* do. Here, in part, was the answer. However, the key to this state of affairs was good VFR weather and light winds.

After lunching and sunbathing on the sandy shore of the lake, we fueled up and took off. Ron was in the hot seat while I relaxed in the back. "Relax" would not accurately describe my neurotic fear of separation from the ground, but at least I had the opportunity to analyze things. As a mining engineer I felt totally secure with a couple of thousand feet of solid rock overhead, but a couple of thousand feet of fresh air underneath filled me with alarm. I looked out at the wings and knew that they were producing lift—more than a ton of it. But lift, like the air, is invisible. In underground mining nothing survives unless it is made of half-inch steel plate, if then. An aircraft has only a thin aluminum skin. Therefore, assuming that this absurd structure were to continue its mad career through the hot, bumpy sky, there was no apparent reason why it should not disintegrate and no certainty that it was not about to do so. The fact that thousands of these things were flying about, and had been doing so for years without falling apart, was something the irrational interior of my mind did not accept.

We returned by way of Keremeos and Hedley, up the headwaters of the Ashnola River, and across to the Hope-Princeton highway. We threaded our way down the valley to a touch-and-go landing at Hope, and climbed away toward Victoria. The sun was sliding down the western sky as we approached Vancouver Island. It is always a privilege to approach "the Island" and, some would say, to leave the real world behind. In company with several other airplanes, we joined the Victoria traffic circuit. The world became quieter and slower as we taxied in to the Flying Club. We left our faithful aircraft to sleep its sleep and dream whatever dreams airplanes go in for, wandered bemusedly into the clubhouse, settled our accounts, and went our separate ways.

The Victoria Flying Club private pilot course contained two

navigation exercises under dual instruction, known as "Nav. 1" and "Nav. 2." Doug reckoned that I had completed the equivalent of Nav. 1, and the following evening we took off for Nav. 2.

The air was clear and still, a beautiful August evening. We took IMH, a friendly airplane, but not a high performer, as we were to discover. East of Victoria airport lay two chains of islands separated by a channel. I had flown this way the day before, so map reading was easy until Doug asked me to identify the islands which lay spread out before us. A different set of islands lined up in a different direction to show a similar open channel. Hadn't thought of that.

We came to the mainland shore, called Abbotsford tower on the radio, and started our descent. Runway 18 was shorter and narrower than the runways at Victoria and, when I tried to land on it, I dropped us in to a real, pre-solo-style hard landing right in front of the tower. My blushing ears bathed the undersides of the wings with a red glow as we climbed away to visit someone else.

The next stop was Langley, where the runway was about the width of a garden path. We taxied back past the flight line, inspecting people and airplanes and being inspected in turn. We backtracked to the farthest end of the runway, swung around, and blasted off. The runway was short as well as narrow; we ran out of blacktop at an alarming rate. My attempts to drag us off the ground did not help. Doug took control, coaxed the aircraft into the air, and wafted us over some tall trees conveniently situated off the end of the runway. That runway was 2,100 feet long; we used 2,099 feet. No, that's an exaggeration. We only used 2,098 feet. Two pairs of lungs let out a long sigh of relief when we were at last clear of the obstructions.

Doug sprung a surprise by telling me to "divert" to Boundary Bay, an old wartime airfield recently refurbished to lure small airplanes away from Vancouver International. Complete with control tower, it lay on a desolate marsh by the sea. It was only 5 minutes away, and I feverishly thumbed through the VFR Chart Supplement (the Canadian airport directory) to look up the runway layout, radio frequencies, and such. I got it all wrong, Doug had to steer me in the right direction. A solitary Cessna was doing circuits and landings, quietly minding its own business. Otherwise the place was deserted. Once more we hit the ground with a hefty thud, took off over the muddy shoreline, and climbed away over the water.

We set course for the gray-black islands heaped on a metallic sea as they faded into the western ocean's dusk. The airport lights were already twinkling as we turned onto final approach.

Navigation was up to requirements, but it was a fitting scene for what must occur to every student as he and his instructor disentangle themselves from the aircraft.

Instructor: "Any questions?"

Student: "Yes. How do you fly an airplane?"

—11—

Up Island

After first solo the next major achievement for the student pilot is the first solo cross-country flight away from home base. The route specified by the Victoria Flying Club ran up the east coast of Vancouver Island to Campbell River, a distance of 110 nautical miles each way.

At the beginning of September, Doug declared that I was ready for this adventure; indeed he pressed me to get on with it before the autumnal foul weather set in. Therefore, some three weeks after the two navigation exercises, I decided to make the trip one Saturday. I promptly learned lesson #1 of VFR cross-country flying: You cannot "decide" to be at any specific place at any specific time or date. The weather on the appointed day was gray and overcast with low, dragging clouds, resulting in lesson #2: cancellation before the flight. Lesson #3, cancellation during the flight, or the 180° turn, was soon to follow.

Tuesday, September 13, dawned clear and bright. I sneaked a day off work and telephoned the weatherman at 7:30 A.M. A weak cold front was due to reach Campbell River about noon, with poorer weather following on behind. "It's so weak you probably won't even notice it," said he blithely. I reckoned that I could get to Campbell River and back out again before the front, and high-tailed it to the airport. ZLG was available. I fueled it up, submitted my navigation plan to Doug for approval, filed my flight plan, and preflighted the aircraft. Even so, it was 10:30 before I took off, full of apprehensions of the unknown.

The first checkpoint on the route was Active Pass, a narrow channel of whirlpools and tide rips between Mayne and Galiano islands. I followed a ferry boat, climbing steadily.

Even in a small airplane perspectives of time and distance are altered amazingly. The ferry passes along a watery avenue between islands whose lofty peaks raise their heads to the clouds. Here is a long view up a sound, a tiny harbor at its head, there a rocky islet with a solitary cottage half hidden in the trees. In an aircraft the islands were right on our doorstep; we climbed above the highest in a few minutes. To navigate, we compared the shapes on our charts with those laid out so conveniently beneath us. The ferry boats with their pounding diesels took 45 minutes from Active Pass to dock at Swartz Bay, the ferry terminal for Victoria. When we were inbound over "the Pass," it was 5 minutes or so between making initial radio contact with the tower and joining the circuit.

As I now set course northward along the islands, a layer of broken cloud prevented me from climbing above 4,500 feet. I talked to the Flight Service Station at Nanaimo and was soon looking down at the town.

Flying on over Nanoose Bay, it became evident that all was not well ahead. The air turned rough, and cumulus clouds lay draped over the mountains. Flying the aircraft was a full-time job, and I dispensed with the niceties of time-and-distance checks. Soon I was weaving between clouds and dropping down to 3,000 feet. Ducking under a cloud, I could see the front directly over Courtenay, barring my route to Campbell River. Woolly gray clouds lay on the mountains. The sky was clear over the straits, but a bed of cloud lay between the shore and the mountains. It was temptingly clear on top of the cloud, but underneath was a greenish-gray mass of rain.

Thinking that, if I flew out of the sunlight under the cloud's shadow, I would be able to see through the rain, I tried to duck beneath the cloud deck. Approaching its edge, I was down to 1,100 feet and needed to go still lower. I could see only a drab landscape fading into the rain. With a sudden choking sensation, I realized that this was no mere classroom exercise. Here was an all too real weather situation which I did not believe I could penetrate safely. Unless I rolled into an immediate steep turn, I would drown in that lethal vapor, which even now was surging toward me. Applying full throttle, I did so without further ado, missing the cloud by a matter of feet. Another Cessna flew past me, boring on into the gloom, but that was his affair.

I fancied a stop and a leg-stretch at Comox. Comox was a military airfield, but I had heard civilian-registered aircraft talking to the tower on the radio and evidently landing there, so why should I not do so? The control tower seemed remarkably uncooperative and, after a conversation at cross-purposes, I asked for permission to land, which was refused.

With foul weather in one direction and a hostile control tower in another, there was no alternative but to head for home.

The front was spilling over the mountains and the turbulence was worse. Near Nanaimo the air became smoother, and I continued at high speed. ZLG had long-range fuel tanks, and it was fortunate that I had started out with full ones. I had flown most of the way to my destination and all the way back again. It was my longest solo flight to date: 2 hours 25 minutes.

The people at the Flying Club were surprised to see me back so soon. When I explained myself, they were glad to have their fledgling and their aircraft back in one piece. To satisfy course requirements, however, I would have to do it all over again—and get there.

The cold front lost all its huff and puff as it left the mountains. Later that afternoon all that was left was a line of small white clouds drifting away over the Straits of Juan de Fuca.

A week later the weather was so fine that I decided to take another shot at reaching Campbell River. Canceled once before the flight, and once during the flight, the third attempt had to be the lucky one. After the last performance I was thoroughly apprehensive, even though a high-pressure weather system lay fair and square over Vancouver Island.

When I reached the airport, one of our aviatrices was flying ZLG on her first solo. She was a little wispy girl who had reached this point after long and determined effort. I went out to the corner of the hangar to watch her land. She flared out too high and dropped the airplane in with a clang that could be heard plumb across the airfield. I preflighted the plane with much care. I wanted to pick it up and shake it to see if it rattled. I whispered in its ear to ask if it was all right.

There was not a cloud in the cold, crystal-clear sky. At 6,500 feet the temperature was just at freezing. Eastward across the water lay a smoggy Vancouver. The Coast Ranges were capped with the first snows of autumn. To the west lay the tangled mountains of the Vancouver Island interior.

I reflected on the phenomenon of flight and could find no answer. I was a mile above the ground in an absurd structure supposedly upheld on things sticking out of it. I was strapped into a seat surrounded by a skin of aluminum so thin that I could almost poke finger holes in it. The structure was pushed and pulled in various directions by unseen forces. It perched on an unseen piece of sky. Ahead was an endless succession of similar pieces of sky, all invisible, which would presumably continue

to support it. The engine would presumably go on running. Presumably
the thing would not disintegrate. Presumably it would continue to
respond to my control pressures as it had for a good many previous
hours of flight. Having always felt perfectly secure in underground
mines, I was full of nervous, fluttery, embarrassed feelings bordering
on plain terror when surrounded by all this space. It was agoraphobia
and acrophobia at the same time. There was nothing to be done about
it, so I tiptoed on across the sky.

Campbell River airport showed up from miles away as a black
runway and some buildings in a featureless tract of bush. The Flight
Service Station was as clear as a bell on the radio, and quite soon I was
looking down at the airfield from the traffic pattern.

The approach and landing were the climax of the journey so far. I
had found my way here; now for the first time I was to land by myself
on a strange runway. Under the intense concentration I was no longer
flying the aircraft; I *was* the aircraft. I was too busy lining up on an
unfamiliar airfield even to look at the instruments. I threw the numbers
into the slipstream and flew so that it felt right. Sure enough, it was right.
My eyes gave me altitude, heading, and attitude; my ears gave me
airspeed and rpm; my hands, toes, and the seat of my pants gave me
everything else. Keeping enough airspeed to slice through the thermals
rising from the bush, I rumbled and bumped down the approach path to
a passable landing.

I turned off at the apron and stopped beside the gas pump. The
pleasant factotum came out, and we gave ZLG a drink. He pointed me
to a parking spot on a patch of gravel. Sitting gratefully on the aircraft's
wheel, I dug some lunch out of my bag and ate. The Flying Club had
entrusted me with this expensive and delicate piece of equipment to fly
it to a far-off place and bring it safely back again. So far I had succeeded.

I filed a new flight plan in the Flight Service Station, pushed and
pulled ZLG onto the asphalt, swept the ground beneath its nose so that
stones would not fly up and nick the propeller, and was soon on my way.
Part of the exercise was to land at Nanaimo. The approach and landing
at an unfamiliar airport is always a problem for the novice pilot. The
thing is a different size and shape from the home patch, and the
surroundings are different. The instrument pilot has an "approach
plate," which tells him exactly where he is supposed to be at each stage
in the approach, how high, and pointing in what direction. When flying
visually, the pilot has a similar approach plate, although a subconscious
one, for each airfield and runway which he already knows, as well as

an unconscious procedure for sizing up an airfield which he does not know. Both of these are based on experience, which the novice pilot has yet to develop.

Having muffed the approach at Nanaimo, I thud-screeched onto the ground. The locals eyed me with suspicion as I taxied back past the flight line. I was soon back on the runway and headed for Victoria. ZLG climbed like a winged brick in the hot bumpy air, following an inlet of the sea between forested hills. We were forthwith back in familiar territory near Duncan. The Saanich Peninsula was veiled in haze and the smoke from slash fires.* Indeed at this time of year haze and smoke could be quite a problem for visual flight. Not long afterward I was taxiing in to the Flying Club. I whispered thanks in the airplane's ear before leaving it to snooze in the afternoon sun.

---

* "Slash" is the scrap material left behind by logging operations. In the Pacific Northwest it is commonly piled up and burned after the first rain of autumn.

12

Going for a Spin

Spins are not a compulsory part of the private pilot training syllabus in the United States, but they are in Canada. The Canadian private pilot flight test candidate is required "to enter and recognize the incipient stage of a spin and to use immediate and correct control applications to accomplish recovery with the minimum loss of altitude." This must be demonstrated to the examiner. Nothing says the candidate must spin or have spun solo, alone in a madly gyrating sky. But there are those who do and those who do not. No one says anything; no one knows. Only the pilot knows whether, having run his finger along the fine edge of his terror and felt the sharpness of it, he has grasped it in his hand and crushed it, or whether he has drawn back unbloodied into an uneasy truce.

I had been pestering Doug to teach me spins, not because I wanted any part of the beastly things, but because they had to be done. We had never got around to it. Doug had taken a well-earned vacation, and I arranged a lesson with Craig Alguire, the Chief Flying Instructor and Club Manager. Craig was a spruce, dapper individual, a former Air BC pilot. We eyed each other with certain misgivings, which evaporated as soon as we climbed into an airplane.

We took IDS, a Cessna 150 beefed up for aerobatics. It was a little frayed at the edges and had massive shoulder harnesses instead of the usual car-type belts, jettisonable doors, and no artificial horizon or direction gyro. It seemed to be in all respects a rugged, macho airplane. It would probably break rocks with its teeth and spit out the pieces. The airplanes all had their characters. ZLG was new and shiny. If you were good, it liked you; if you were not so good, it tolerated you. IMH was the friendly airplane that rattled; it licked your face when you said hello to it before a flight. UZR had a warped sense of humor; it specialized in strange electrical faults. I was about to make the acquaintance of IDS.

We took off and climbed to 4,000 feet over Shawnigan Lake while Craig quizzed me about various things on the way. He told me to demonstrate slow flight and some stalls. I explained my poor performance by pointing out that I had not practiced these things because I had not learned spins. Slow flight and stalls could both lead to spins. He admitted that that made sense.

There were mean-looking gray clouds overhead and knobbly mountains below. Nevertheless, this was obviously where it was about to happen. I knew that I was about to be utterly terrified and that there was no escape. It was worse than a dental appointment. In half an hour the lesson would be over and both feet would be on *terra firma*. The interval was going to be most unpleasant.

Craig demonstrated the first spin out of a stalled steep turn. The aircraft stopped in mid-air, rolled over onto its back, and headed earthward. The gyrating landscape, the swooshing of wind, the rising wail of the stall warning, the creaking of the aircraft, all filled me with terror. With such an uninterrupted view of the ground as it whirled like a roulette wheel before my eyes, I had a feeling of not being in an aircraft at all. IDS wound itself into the spin, producing an appalling sensation of being sucked down a vortex. When every hair on my head was fully upright and emitting enough sparks to black out radio reception within 5 miles, Craig recovered from the spin and the g force crushed us down into our seats as he pulled out of the resulting vertiginous dive. He demonstrated this unspeakable maneuver once or twice more and we headed for home.

The mystery was how a normal, well-mannered little airplane could have such a Jekyll-and-Hyde personality. It would take off, climb, turn, fly straight and level, and otherwise behave in an orderly manner. Yet it would also perform this ghastly maneuver that bore no resemblance to flight at all.

"OK," said Craig, once we were back on the ground, "when do you want to book your next lesson?"

"How about Tuesday evening?"

"Spins?"

"Yup," I replied obstinately and walked away. It was several hours before my hair lay down flat.

The evenings were beginning to draw in and dusk was not far off when we met for another lesson in IDS. This time Craig briefed me in detail on how an aircraft spins and why. I still wonder if anyone really knows. I knew for sure that a great many things happened at once, all of them thoroughly unpleasant.

As we climbed into the evening sky, Craig said, "Now, can you take me to the Victoria VOR?" (The aircraft had a VOR set.) Witlessly I replied, "Sure, it's on that hill over there." Not what was meant at all.

After climbing continuously for 15 miles, we reached the colossal height of 5,000 feet over Duncan. The sky was cloudless; the air still. We got right into the spins—entry, one turn, recovery. After I had done a few by my own unaided efforts, Craig said, "OK, you've got that pretty well. Now we'll look at some aggravated stalls." I knew I was going to have to spin by myself and wanted to get used to the sensation while there was still an instructor in the other seat. Furthermore, I had just had my fill of abnormal flight maneuvers and was not interested in aggravated stalls. Craig sat back in boredom while I spun and spun. Then it was time to go home. I insisted on showing off a fancy pattern that I used to practice steep turns. IDS handled slightly differently from the 152s and the maneuver came unglued, much to my embarrassment.

Craig said: "Now *I'm* going to show *you* something." We started a shallow dive until the airspeed built up to 115 knots. Then the g force pressed us into our seats as Craig pulled the nose up into the Prussian blue sky of dusk. Up and up we went over the top of a loop, still firmly in our seats even though inverted. The flame-red band of the western sky fell across the windshield, followed by the green-black hills, the outlines of fields blurred in the summer dusk, and finally the familiar shape of the Saanich Peninsula right side up. We hit our own wake with a slight jolt. I was hooked on aerobatics from that moment.

We asked the tower controller to give us a practice DF homing. Some control towers have equipment that indicates the bearing of an aircraft's radio transmission, from which they can give a lost pilot headings to steer, which will bring him to the airport. The tower earnestly adjured us to "maintain VFR at all times." Because there was not a cloud within a hundred miles, we complied without undue difficulty. The runway lights were twinkling in the gathering darkness as we floated in to land.

My next solo flight had to include spins. I could almost squirt sweat from the palms of my hands merely by thinking about it. My insides knotted themselves into new and hitherto untried configurations or revolved like the crankshaft of a marine diesel. The first time I took off for an appointment with destiny, the smoke from slash fires filled the

Cowichan Valley up to 3,000 feet. I was not about to risk spinning down into the smoke and declared chicken.

Solo spins obsessed me. As a mine foreman in Colorado, had I not walked through the passageways of a haunted mine alone at night, knowing it to be haunted, with no more concern than wondering what the night's spectral exhibitions would bring forth? Had I not escaped death underground by a hair's breadth many times and laughed it off? But spins? People have their limits, and perhaps I had reached mine. Perhaps I was not pilot material and had struggled on this far without realizing it. Perhaps this was the time to look facts in the face. I took off in UZR for solo spins.

The evening was clear and still—no excuses this time. At 5,000 feet I thought how nice the world looked right side up and what a pity it was to disturb it. I went through the necessary checks meticulously. Then I spun. Certainly there was the jab of fear like a fist in the stomach, but I came out of the first one without difficulty, and then five more. UZR spun slowly and with intense concentration, and stopped spinning in the same fashion when asked to. UZR would always help out in a pinch. When things were not in a pinch, or when it thought the pilot needed sharpening up, it exercised its bizarre sense of humor.

My fear of flying broke up like chunks of ice. I twisted the airplane's tail and it laughed. I told it to spin and it spun; I told it to stop spinning and it did so. I was treading on thin air, playing tunes on the stall warning, and pretending to be a dive-bomber. I was some kind of a pilot. To be afraid of flight was not only unnecessary; it was absurd. Armed with this new insight, I approached the private pilot flight test.

—13————————

Judgment Day

Craig Alguire had been remarking that I was ready for the flight test. I arranged to take it on the first day of October. On the day before the test, I took time off work for the traditional pre-test checkout. Craig put me through the hoops with an oral exam, which revealed some alarming deficiencies. He reckoned that a flight was unnecessary. I disagreed.

Martin Tucker insisted on taking my photograph while I was fueling ZLG. Better pilots than I have discovered that it is bad luck to be photographed before a flight. Protestations and abuse were unavailing, and in the end I allowed him to take the photograph. They also say that it is good and necessary to make a hash of the pre-test check ride because it sharpens the candidate's wits for the real thing.

Craig and I took off and headed southward. It was scorching hot, and the air was full of bumps. As soon as we reached 2,000 feet, Craig announced that the engine had just failed. I spotted a windsock on a patch of grass but, apart from the fact that I omitted all the essential procedures, I made such a mess of things that we abandoned the exercise. Craig was not pleased, but it was a comedy of errors. Craig had started the exercise within gliding distance of a small airstrip which I had not seen. I had locked onto the windsock with the idea that windsocks and airfields went together like bacon and eggs. My windsock belonged to a parachute landing ground, and we had been at cross-purposes ever since.

On the next day I reported for the test. A certain degree of nervousness is not only justifiable, it is a good thing. The commercial and instrument flight tests are more demanding, but they are not as significant as the private pilot flight test. The candidate, if successful, becomes a licensed pilot at that point. That is when he wins his wings. Not least among the nervous ones are the candidate's instructor and the chief flying instructor of the school. If a significant number of candidates recommended by an instructor fail the flight test, the instructor's qualification comes under scrutiny. The flight test scores reflect the effectiveness of the school itself.

The government inspector is a pilot with many years of professional flying behind him. He probably knows the flying school and the instructors well, yet he must be perfectly impartial. His responsibility is heavy. If a newly licensed pilot flies into a mountain (or performs some equivalent act where there are no mountains), the question is heard like a thunderclap: *"Who passed him on his flight test?"*

At the time I had other and more pressing concerns than these. The day before the flight test I had been told to plan a flight from Victoria to Powell River in a Cessna 152 with two people and 80 lb of baggage.

On the day of the test, the weather was calm, but the pinkish gray smoke of slash fires hung thickly in the lower air. The examiner was John Addison, a former Chief Flying Instructor with the Flying Club, employed by the British Columbia government to fly Cessna Citations and other complex, high-performance aircraft. John was an Englishman who could be followed by the trail of matches spent in the unending attempt to light his pipe. Indeed, John had fought a running battle with his employer about pipe smoking in the cockpit of a bizjet. He had previously flown Vulcans with the "Lincolnshire Air Force," as RAF Bomber Command came to be known. His slightly languid air was enough to put the most nervous candidate at ease. It was impossible to look him in the eye without agreeing that most of life is an unexpressed joke.

The test began with a searching oral examination which put the proposed flight under a magnifying glass and dissected its planning and intended execution. The questioning moved on to the aircraft, its flight, the numbers, the systems, the airframe—always followed up by: "Why?" Finally: "Why do the ailerons have lead weights in them?" I had to admit that I never knew there were lead weights in the ailerons, but I supposed they would be there to damp out flutter. For a fleeting moment I had the feeling that here were not an examiner and examinee but two pilots (yes, *two* pilots) kicking a few things around and discussing the strange ways of flight.

At length we sauntered out into the office to wait for ZLG to come back. In the end we decided to take IMH instead. I preflighted it, including the lead weights in the ailerons, while John looked on and gurgled with his pipe. We climbed in, started up, and taxied out.

"Supposing the cloud was at 5,500 feet," said John. "What would you do?"

"Our cruising altitude to Powell River just became 4,500 feet instead of 6,500," I replied.

"Now," said he, "the runway surface is six inches of wet grass." I put on 10° of flap. When we were cleared for takeoff, he told me to hold the power back to 2,000 rpm to simulate the effect of the grass. We had 6,000 feet of asphalt in front of us and must have used 4,000 feet before lifting off. We applied full throttle and climbed away.

We climbed on course with Saltspring Island off our right wing. Once above the smoke, the air was clear. We leveled off at 4,500 feet, and the smoke plume from the mill at Crofton showed up ahead as our set-heading point. I leaned the mixture and trimmed the aircraft. John told me to do a time-and-distance check on my circular slide rule and gave the rudder a furtive kick while I was thus occupied, to see how quickly I noticed that we had slewed off course.

At that point we abandoned the cross-country flight and started the maneuvers. A power-off stall came first, followed by a recovery into a glide. I remembered to do the checks known by the mnemonic HASEL before starting the maneuver—no HASEL check, fail the test. Next came a full-power stall out of a climbing turn, slow flight with 90° turns, a steep turn at 70 knots, a spin. We were wandering southward over Duncan, and John asked for the spin directly over the town. I suggested that we do it somewhere else. The penalty for doing an aerobatic maneuver over a built-up area would be to fail the test. One student failed for flying less than 500 feet below a cloud. Oh yes, there are many pitfalls, and the candidate had better have all his wits about him.

"Now," said John, "you see black smoke coming from under the engine cowling." I ran my fingers over the switches, pretending, for the purposes of the exercise, to switch the engine off. In fact I did no such thing. The engine remained ticking over and, indeed, the candidate was expected to remember to open the throttle once every thousand feet of descent to ensure that the simulation did not turn into reality, as has happened on numerous occasions in the past. Fuel off, mixture to idle cutoff, ignition off, set up a fast glide, and try to blow out the "fire." That seemed to do it because the "black smoke" disappeared. I now had to carry out a practice forced approach from more than 3,000 feet with plenty of time to think about it. Duncan airstrip beckoned like the cheese on a mousetrap, but I had told John that I would land in a grass field rather than go into Duncan.

This time I had to call the shot and say where we were going to land and in which direction. I turned onto final approach to the chosen field too high and too close. A healthy sideslip dropped us into place. Suddenly I noticed that a 90° turn would set us up nicely for a much better field; there was no wind. I said what I was going to do, made the turn, hung out the flaps, and there we were. At about 200 feet above the ground, John told me to overshoot. I applied full throttle and we climbed away.

After we had regained 1,000 feet, the next question was to work out a course, distance, and estimated time of arrival to go to Abbotsford. When I had produced the answers to these questions, we followed the shoreline of Cowichan Bay to a small grass airstrip known as the Jackson Strip. John had said that we might actually land on a grass airstrip, so perhaps this was it.

The airstrip was two ruts beside a limp windsock. First I decided to land one way, then changed my mind. I made a series of sloppy attempts to line up in a regular pattern. In the end I organized a ragged, misaligned final approach. Having wandered over a substantial area of ground, I felt that by now I should be producing results. A sharp sideslip, power off, and full flaps produced the desired effect. The smooth rumble of wheels on the grass was only a second away when John said, "Overshoot!" Full power, carb heat cold, reestablish flight, flaps 10°, lift over the trees ahead, pull in the flaps, and keep going.

"Let's go home," said John. We climbed to 1,500 feet and swung round over Cowichan Bay to fit the inbound traffic pattern. We were on the downwind leg for runway 26 when John took the microphone and asked for a landing clearance on runway 20. Said he, "You're cleared to land on runway 20; hold short of 26." That gave me about 1,500 feet of runway in which to flare out, land, and stop. I was about 10 knots too fast on final approach, and we floated forever before plunking down. There was no point in burning up the brakes so we careened across runway 26. "Oh well," said John philosophically, "Get stopped somewhere before the end of the runway."

We taxied in and tied the aircraft down. John wandered around it lighting his pipe and inspecting small dents in its hide. The burning question remained unanswered. We went into the back office. He put various checkmarks on a scoresheet, all from memory. At long last he said: "Congratulations." We shook hands.

To pass the flight test is to be told by someone completely impartial, whose word carries real weight: "You've made the grade. You're a pilot." When a student wins his wings, there is a subtle change in the way people treat him where he does his flying. The student pilot is on probation, and there is a washout rate of one sort and another. The proportion of "temporary faces" is high. The "permanent faces" reserve their approbation. The aspirant must establish himself as a person of mature judgment who will treat expensive aircraft with care. The new pilot is still a very junior member of the aviation fraternity and does well to keep his mouth shut, but he has shown the courage and determination to win his wings, and the fraternity quietly pats him on the back.

—14

On the Gauges

Autumn passed; winter set in with a vengeance. Weather systems in endless variety came storming in from the North Pacific, stirred to fury by impact with Canada's mountainous coastline. Clouds and mists and shifting fogbanks covered land and sea alike. Drenching rains hammered into the sodden ground. Wild winds swept the sky clean from time to time, but in either event the winter sky was uninviting to the newly fledged pilot of a small airplane, and for much of the time was forbidden territory.

At that time my job demanded unremitting attention during the week. Short days restricted flying to weekends. Foul weather could keep me grounded for weeks on end. My still meager proficiency was not improving.

We had been warned of the disastrous consequences of entering cloud without instrument training. "Cloud" to me meant white, puffy cumulus floating in a blue sky. Who could be so crass as to fly into one unintentionally?

One November afternoon I approached the airport in my car from the south as foul weather rolled in from the north. I hurriedly preflighted IDS, anxious to get airborne if only to fly once around the airport. Even as I ran my hand over the aircraft's familiar exterior, I kept watching the sky. The cloud ceiling sank lower; the visibility grew less.

"Tower, India Delta Sierra ready for takeoff."

"India Delta Sierra, roger. Do you have an instructor on board?"

"Negative."

"India Delta Sierra, you're cleared for takeoff for one circuit only."

"India Delta Sierra, I was thinking that very thing."

I leveled off at 500 feet as a mistiness around me indicated that the indistinct cloud base was only just above. On the downwind leg of the circuit, I had only the airfield at my left elbow as a horizon. The islands to the east had disappeared. With incredible suddenness cloud was racing beneath me, and for a split second I was inside it. By the utmost good fortune blue-gray water appeared below, and I whisked into a diving turn toward it. I popped out into the clear on base leg for the runway, skidded around onto final approach, and landed thankfully.

One of the groundschool instructors had preached The Word about a night endorsement, partly for its utility and partly for the basic instrument training that went with it. I had listened with half an ear because at the time I was having great difficulty in flying by day. Why would I want to fly at night? Who but an idiot would fly into a cloud without meaning to anyway? The winter of 1983-84 brought abundant answers to these questions.

One winter evening, after the weather had rained and stormed itself to exhaustion, I stepped out of my back door to see a full moon riding quietly in a clear sky. Flying conditions were obviously ideal, and only the lack of a night endorsement was keeping me on the ground. If I could not fly by day, I would do so by night. The clincher was that the Flying Club was offering a night flying course for a lump sum at a discount. I approached Doug one afternoon and asked if he would like to teach me to fly in the dark. The answer being in the affirmative, we made the necessary arrangements forthwith.

We have already seen in passing that the visual pilot relies totally on orientating himself by reference to the ground. If he is cut off from a clear indication of which way is up, only a trained interpretation of the aircraft's instruments can save him from destruction at his own hands. The senses other than sight are worse than useless; they are misleading. They never suggest anything useful such as a minor deviation in heading or altitude. They always scream disaster. The aircraft can be in straight and level flight, yet out they come yelling that it is in a steep bank, a climb, dive, roll, or spin. Yet when the aircraft is in an attitude from which loss of control is imminent, they sit back and say nothing.

When deprived of outside visual references for more than a few seconds, the pilot without instrument training will die in one of three maneuvers. He may survive if the airframe stands up to it and if he breaks out of cloud more than 2,000 feet above ground, but those factors are often missing. The three maneuvers are the roller coaster, the spiral dive, and the spin.

It is sometimes said, "If you end up in cloud accidentally, set up a glide, keep the aircraft straight, and cross your fingers." If the pilot is really lucky, there may be a chance that he will survive unless the roller coaster gets him. If an aircraft is properly trimmed in level flight, a climb, or a descent, it will tend to stay that way as long as the power setting remains unchanged. If a wind gust, control movement, or other disturbance makes it nose up or down, it will try to return to its trimmed attitude and will hunt for it in a slow, porpoising motion called a "phugoid." The period of the aircraft's natural phugoid is quite long— long enough to tempt the pilot to interfere.

Clouds are often bumpy inside, and in instrument conditions the pilot's ears become abnormally sensitive to changes in aircraft noise. Suppose that the pilot without instrument training is in cloud accidentally and is established in straight and level flight or in a glide to get down out of cloud. He detects a faint change in airspeed. He corrects by raising or lowering the nose and the airspeed starts to go the other way. He overcorrects slightly and back it goes again. He is immediately into a positive feedback situation of steeper and steeper climbs and descents and away to the funeral.

I started my instrument training with several roller coasters in a simulator with the roll and yaw functions turned off, with the lid open, in a lighted room, with an instructor looking over my shoulder. If I had been in a small aircraft in turbulent cloud, the possible results can be left to imagination.

The spiral dive is a natural tendency of some aircraft, especially if they are slightly out of balance to one side or the other. If a pilot flies by himself in a Cessna 152 straight and level, and then takes his hands and feet off the controls, it will, in less than a minute, begin gently to sneak off into a lefthand spiral. The aircraft is so delicately balanced that he can sometimes prevent it from doing so by nothing more than leaning over onto the righthand seat. The beginning is so slow and gentle that in normal flight the pilot never lets it start. The visual pilot in cloud, however, will not feel the early stages, and by the time he does notice, the process is well launched. Because the maneuver is self-reinforcing (another positive feedback situation) things will be happening quite rapidly by then, even with no input from the pilot. He senses that he is going down faster and faster in a straight dive and hauls back on the yoke, which is like trying to put out a fire with gasoline. Witnesses report pieces of aircraft falling out of the cloud.

If our late and misguided pilot had got himself into a spin, and even if he had had the presence of mind to get out of it, his senses would have fooled him that he was still in it, with the result that he would have corrected himself into a spin in the opposite direction, unless the aircraft went into a spiral dive in the process. The final result is equally distressing either way.

Some of the early pilots tell us in their memoirs that they did fly blind through cloud with nothing more than a few simple instruments. The vista which greeted them in the cloudy canyons or above the clouds had never before been seen by mortal eye, except by a few balloonists. It soon became known, however, that even though a few pilots did fly successfully through cloud with only those few instruments, and perhaps some continued to do so, for most pilots it was extremely dangerous. The assertion that it can be done is not worth testing.

At night, clouds can be flown into before they are seen. Ground lights can be so few as to be misleading, or they can be entirely absent over water or uninhabited country. The pilot cannot be let loose into the night sky without knowing how to fly by instruments. Herein, too, lies a trap. It has been found that the small amount of instrument flying taught for the night endorsement imparts a skill which lapses from disuse. After all, the training is for an eventuality that the cunning pilot will do everything in his power to avoid. If he is successful, he never has occasion to fly by instruments, except in the initial climb, until that moment when an unseen cloud lies in his path. Deeper training and regular practice are needed to produce a pilot capable of controlling the aircraft in that distant eventuality.

The tragedy of pilots killed while trying to fly without external visual references is that they often had the necessary information staring at them out of their instrument panels, but they had not been taught how to organize it. The fledgling instrument pilot must learn not only to organize the true information being fed to him by the instruments but also to fight down the weird, frightening, and, above all, false information fed to him by his own bodily senses.

So what is this Big Deal, this "flying by instruments," or "blind flying," as it used to be called? The visual pilot knows that he has a panel full of instruments staring at him. Sometimes he uses some of them to check on what the aircraft is doing, but his basic instrumentation is that of the bird. Many visual pilots pride themselves on how little they need the instruments. But when the familiar references are not there any more, it is a different story.

There are six basic blind flying instruments. Three are driven by gyroscopes: the artificial horizon, heading indicator, and turn indicator.

Three are driven by air pressures: the airspeed indicator, altimeter, and vertical speed indicator.

A gyroscope, when spinning, maintains its attitude in space and resists attempts to change that attitude. In a Cessna light aircraft one gyroscope is driven by a DC electric motor fed from the electrical system. Two others are driven by a vacuum pump driven directly by the engine.

The DC gyroscope drives the turn indicator. This instrument indicates the rate of change of the aircraft's heading with the rate-one turn as a reference. A "rate-one turn" means a change of heading of 3° per second, or 180° in a minute. This is a gentle and convenient rate of turn used as a standard in instrument flight.

One vacuum-driven gyroscope drives the attitude indicator (sometimes known as the artificial horizon), which simultaneously shows the aircraft's attitude in pitch and roll (nose up or down, left or right bank). The other vacuum gyroscope drives the heading indicator. The aircraft's magnetic compass flops and swirls in its case in response to turbulence, turns, and accelerations and is therefore not an accurate means of holding a heading in blind conditions. The heading indicator is, in effect, a gyrostabilized compass. In its basic form, however, it will not seek north, and the pilot must therefore set it by reference to the magnetic compass. Precession of the gyroscope causes the heading indicator to creep out of adjustment, and for real accuracy the pilot must reset it according to the magnetic compass every 15 or 20 minutes.

The airspeed indicator compares the pressure of the undisturbed air with the impact pressure of the air through which the aircraft is pushing its way. The altimeter is little more than an aneroid barometer calibrated to read altitude as the barometric pressure decreases with increasing height. A setting knob allows the altimeter to be corrected for changes in sea-level barometric pressure. The vertical speed indicator measures the rate of change of barometric pressure as the aircraft climbs or descends and shows this as a rate of climb or descent in feet per minute.

With the exception of aerobatic flight, in which they cannot respond fast enough or the gyroscopes topple or must be "caged," these instruments describe completely the aircraft's attitude and performance with a measure of built-in redundancy in case a power source fails or a pressure sensor becomes blocked. Controlling the aircraft by instruments in blind flight is a mental process of coordinating the information from these six instruments.

Lesson One on night flying was a session in the instrument flight simulator. The Flying Club had a Frasca in a Holy of Holies upstairs behind a locked door. For once we did not have to worry about the weather. Most people have heard of the computerized miracles whereby a pilot can "fly" a Boeing 747 from New York to Paris or an interception mission in an F-18. The humbler version has been around for much longer and still costs as much as a small airplane. However simple or complex the simulator, the main attractions are low operating costs, freedom from interference by weather and traffic, and the ability to stop the action and discuss what is going on.

The Flying Club's simulator consisted of a generic light aircraft cockpit, a lid to put over the top, and a ground track recorder. In the works was a maze of wiring which would give a telephone technician hysterics, together with mechanical and electrical gadgetry which translated control pressures or movements into instrument readings. Inserting the pupil's eyes (crossed), brain (if functioning), nerves (twitching), hands (sweaty), and feet (of clay) resulted in a feedback loop for the instructor to fool around with to his heart's content.

Doug gave me a short briefing and sat me down in this contraption. After several roller coasters and other wild gyrations, I had the beast under some sort of control. Down came the lid. Doug said that the simulator was set to resemble the Flying Club's twin-engined Piper Seneca. Indeed the controls had a heavy feel to them, and the resulting instrument indications were ponderous. In real flight people like me have to pay close attention to the job in hand, but under the lid my imagination ran wild.

Most people have something in mind as the Ultimate Airplane. Under the lid you can be *anything* and no one will ever know. Some people wish they could be fighter pilots. Not me. Give me a Boeing 747, with a Hercules as second choice. Perhaps I am a multi-engine pilot at heart, but I doubt if I will ever find out.

Doug became any one of a succession of radar approach controllers and I was a 747 making an instrument approach into Chicago on a rainy night. The aircraft lurched as the landing gear extended and locked with multiple clunks. It hung in the sky as the colossal flaps pushed out into the rumbling slipstream. The first orange ground lights shone through the racing clouds. We were 400 feet above ground on final approach when Doug took off the lid and an hour's instruction was over.

We had another session in the simulator. Then it was enough of this foolishness with phony flight. We launch ourselves into the dark sky.

—15

The Dark Sky

By night the weather was even more critical for visual flight than by day. Cloud was invisible unless by moonlight, and windspeeds were harder to judge. With 2,000-foot hills not far away and Mount Newton rising to 1,000 feet just outside the airport traffic circuit, it would not take much wind to blow a small airplane into an unseen mountain. For that reason runway 20 was closed at night. The Pacific coast in winter has its share of wind, rain, and low cloud. At night the temperature and dewpoint merge and ground fog is another hazard. Night flying in the winter merited a good deal of care.

Our first appointment had to be canceled because of low cloud. The next time the weather was slightly better. It was a raw evening, calm, cold, and dark. The red lights on some of the hilltops were already disappearing as the cloud base crept lower. In my thin flying shoes I had cold feet in both senses of the word. My flashlight beam wobbled over ZLG's exterior, outlined dimly by the lights around the control tower. My fingers splashed the icy dew from the leading edges of the wings. The windows were fogged over and resisted my attempts to clear them. I had just about completed the preflight inspection when Doug appeared out of the gloom. We climbed in and shut ourselves into the cold, dead interior of the aircraft.

Everything took twice as long to do. Familiar knobs and switches hid themselves in the shadows. Windows unfogged as the engine warmed up. Having our taxi clearance, we wandered out onto the apron. Each taxiway was edged with blue lights, but, where three taxiways diverged, they lined themselves up into misleading patterns or merged into a uniform carpet. Somewhere a yellow line was supposed to be faintly visible in the glow of a wing-tip navigation light; I had to learn to get by without the landing light. This was awful. Never mind spatial disorientation; I was lost right here on the ground. For a few seconds we sat there with the engine running. I was filled with sudden and large doubts as to my future as a night pilot. Doug coaxed me out onto the correct taxiway, and the blue lights spread out in an avenue ahead.

The engine run-up took many times as long as by day. At last we wheeled out onto the huge, dark runway with its line of white lights on each side, and off we went. As we lifted off, my neck stretched like a turtle's. Doug reminded me to fly immediately and solely by the instruments. Even in clear weather there is a temporary loss of outside references during a night takeoff after the pilot has lost sight of the runway lights and before the aircraft is high enough for him to make sense of the lights on the ground. If the departure is over water or uninhabited country, the loss of outside visual references in the initial climb is complete. Flight by instruments alone is essential, as several pilots have found out to their cost after unwittingly flying back into the ground.

My neck retracted and I hunched over the instruments in the warm red glow of the cockpit lighting. At 500 feet we rolled into a rate-one climbing left turn. I ventured a glance out of the window but was so horrified by the meaningless fuzz of orange ground lights that I returned forthwith to the sanity of the instruments.

Doug told me to stay at 500 feet. A faint note of alarm in his voice told me that we were sliding under the very base of the cloud. He told me when to turn and what course to steer, which I did by the instruments with never a glance outside. Only on base leg did I look out to find that the lights had arranged themselves into a recognizable pattern. The landing which followed was a joint effort.

We took wing again; I locked my gaze onto the instruments at once. This time around Doug liked the weather even less, so we landed and taxied in. Sure enough, I got lost on the ground again.

We taxied in behind the hangar, switched off, and sat in the dark talking about night flying as the mists closed in over the airfield. Less than a year ago I had sat in the same airplane in the same spot, asking Doug if I was pilot material. Now he was teaching me to fly at night.

For a novel experience in aviation, I give you that of making your second night flight in an unfamiliar aircraft in a strong wind. UZR was behind the hangar. The flaps, landing light, and one wingtip light would not work. I went back inside: "I hate to tell you this, Doug, but. . . ." Doug came out and had a look for himself. UZR thought it amusing to have something unserviceable when the pupil checked it but for that item to work perfectly when someone else did so. This time UZR did not want to fly in the dark. The other 152s were tucked up in the hangar behind the 172s.

"You've flown a 172 before, haven't you?" asked Doug.

"Er, well, um, yes-about-last-August-twice-under-dual-instruction."

We pushed IUX out into the night. It sniffed me up and down. It had just gone to sleep and now this.

We fired up and taxied out to runway 13, a sleepy pilot in a sleepy airplane. We lifted off into the night. Compared to a 152, the perspective from a 172 is different, the control pressures are those of a truck. The noises were different, too, and quieter, so that we were often sliding along at 80 knots when we should have been flying an approach at 70. A crosswind was added to this and, in the three circuits we flew, I was completely unable to make a decent approach, let alone land. The invisible black wind tugged and pushed at us out of the night sky.

We climbed away to 4,000 feet over Victoria. My head was stuffed firmly between my shoulders as I flew by instruments following Doug's vectors until he invited me to come up for air and admire the view. To my surprise I could see enough to fly by. The whole of Victoria lay spread out beneath us, blazing with light for our whole and sole amusement, and we reveled in it. Doug pointed out and explained the beacons which winked and flashed all around the horizon.

On went the hood for more instrument practice. The "hood" was a baseball cap with a sheet of aluminum bolted onto the peak so that the pupil's view outside the aircraft was cut off. I had not the least idea where we were going but climbed and turned and descended according to Doug's instructions. Absolute trust of one person in another is a pupil flying under the hood with an instructor.

Off came the hood. "Where are we?" We were over Elk Lake, inbound to the airport. A cloud, faintly luminous in the light of a crescent moon, appeared to hug the ground over Sidney when seen from 3,000 feet. In fact it was more than 1,500 feet from the ground, and we flew a curving descent beneath it. I was more than a little weary and, when Doug told me to get a clearance for circuits from the tower, I groaned inside. I was so tired that I wanted to beg out. But the pilot cannot tell the airplane that he is tired, nor can he fly only when perfectly rested, so I kept my mouth shut.

My next three circuits and landings showed little improvement over my previous performance, so we called it quits. As we switched off outside the hangar, Doug asked in slight surprise: "Do you not find it tiring?" Pouring myself onto the ground, I replied: "Yes, Doug, I find it tiring." (Do you not see my eyeballs hanging off my kneecaps?) We were biting off the training in two-hour chunks, an hour on instruments, an hour on circuits and landings. I was exhausted all the next day.

Five days later we took off at 8:00 P.M. in ZLG and headed for the Duncan practice area. The weather was "twenty-five hundred broken, visibility five miles in light rain showers, temperature 3°C, dewpoint 1°C." In other words, it was a raw evening with low cloud and drizzle. We climbed to the base of the cloud and explored its margins. I reckoned that we would be candidates for airframe ice, but Doug seemed unconcerned. After we had admired the lights of Duncan, on went the hood for flight on the gauges—climbs, descents, timed turns, and how to fly on the remaining instruments if the artificial horizon packs up ("partial panel"), with an introduction to "recovery from unusual attitudes."

If a rate-one turn makes a change of direction of 180° per minute, how many seconds does it take to turn 45°? Elementary arithmetic, but a question that I, a highly trained engineer, could not answer while flying a small airplane at night on instruments.

The mind is so taken up with flying the aircraft and with indefinite fears that the simplest calculation becomes impossible. I knew a fellow who failed his commercial flight test that way. The examiner asked for a timed turn from one heading to another while the candidate was flying by partial panel under the hood. The fellow thought about it for a while, said that he could not do it, and failed the test.

After what seemed like a few minutes Doug took the hood off my head and we had been flying for an hour. Turning toward the airport, we came out from under the cloud deck into the light of a half moon for an hour of circuits and landings. My arrivals were becoming a little more predictable—solid, thud-screech affairs. The people who wrote the how-to-fly books were not around after dark to say that you graduate from headwind landings to crosswind landings, because hitherto all my night landings had been more or less crosswind. Tonight the air was smooth; only a tiny, dark, cold wind drifted us across the approach path, enough to let us turn final a little short and let the wind carry us onto the runway centerline.

We floated down the glidepath. The approach lights were laid out like jewels in black velvet. I felt a sudden and deep realization of flight.

This intense realization is probably slower to arrive than many of us either know or admit. You may reply, "Don't be absurd, of course I know I'm flying." But do you? Do you not manipulate a series of motions and pressures and so cause the normal perspectives of the world to unravel in certain ways? Do you fully and deeply understand that you are not supported on or suspended from anything solid? Do you fully accept both the substance and the insubstantiality of thin air? In the concerns (albeit legitimate and pressing ones) of airspeed and rpm and mixture and carb heat and flaps and fuel and oil pressure and altitude and attitude and heading and ground track and radio frequencies and "India-Mike-Hotel-turn-base-now-keep-it-in-fairly-close-you're-number-two-behind-a-Cessna-172-on-final-caution-possible-wake-turbulence-from-the-Boeing-737-departed-three-minutes-ago," do you fully realize that you are flying?

This realization was so overpowering that I had to wake up abruptly and make a landing as Doug emitted a telepathic expression of concern. Needless to say, the landing that followed was nothing special, because the pilot was doped up on flight.

Doug remarked with the faintest disdain, as the moon sailed up into the sky, that this was just like flying by day. I thought to myself that this was why I wanted a night endorsement. Never mind "twenty-five hundred broken, visibility five miles in light rain showers" and creeping about in the bases of clouds. What I wanted was no cloud at all below cruising altitude, precious little above, and a half moon or better. Such nights were scarce on the Pacific coast in spring.

After we landed, Doug remarked that I would solo on the next flight as by then I would have completed the requisite five hours of night dual. I dismissed this from my tired brain as a figment of imagination. He could not mean that and be in possession of his senses.

Two days later I telephoned Doug before the next lesson to ask for his views on the weather. I lived 30 miles from the airport on the far side of a range of hills, and the weather was often radically different in the two places. Doug said that there was a strong southwesterly wind, making 20 the only usable runway, except that it was closed at night. Further, there was low cloud and the temperature-dewpoint spread was 2°C and closing. It did not take much to see that it was a foul, unflyable night. "Besides," said Doug, "I want you to do some solo and you'll need fairly good conditions." This same crazy idea about solo!

Two days later the weather was better, but it was still pitch dark beneath an overcast. This time ZLG had a navigation light out and we took UZR instead. Having preflighted ZLG first and then UZR, I was flustered as well as tired. Time was getting on. First I forgot a whole section of the checklist and Doug had to remind me. Next I started to taxi with the landing light off, as was standard practice. "Turn right," said Doug with some concern. A black space between the airport lights filled itself in and became a parked aircraft. I would have taxied straight into it. (I have never taxied with the landing light off since!) I was appalled. If the rest of the flight was going to be like this, I might as well abort right now. But perhaps it would be better once airborne. Besides, Doug had taken the trouble to come out and teach me. The least I could do was to stick with it.

Sure enough, when we finally had the aircraft accelerating down the runway, the controls coming alive, and the instruments waking up, everything felt better. We flew south over Victoria. First on the list was recovery on the instruments from oversteepened climbs, overbanked turns, stalls, spiral dives, and the like. Doug told me to close my eyes. Various weaving and wafting motions happened to the aircraft and, when it was in a wild enough attitude: "Open your eyes; you have control." I was able to wrestle the aircraft into some sort of orderly flight without much difficulty. Then there were more climbs and descents, climbing and descending turns, stalls, spirals, and similar evolutions. Off with the hood: "Where are we?" It was time for circuits and thuds.

Turning downwind for the umpteenth time after yet another thud-screech arrival, I thought: "I must be crazy. I'm bone-weary. I let myself get shut up in this little itty-bitty putt-putt airplane flying around up here in the dark. And here's this other guy. He must be crazy, too, because he's done this ten million times and still he comes out and does it some more when we could both be sitting in our respective armchairs drinking beer." Doug said, "Make this a full-stop landing." An alarm bell rang in my mind. I had heard that tone in his voice before, and it meant, "I'm going to send you solo." This idea was so improbable that I dismissed it as an illusion.

We landed and taxied in. Doug said, "Well, you're ready to take it up by yourself." I jumped. "You really think so?" The answer being in the affirmative, Doug climbed out with instructions to do one touch-and-go landing and then to land, and left me to my own devices. I had been tired to begin with. After an hour on instruments and half an hour of circuits, I was really exhausted. Besides, how on earth am I supposed to fly this creature in the dark? I looked around the cockpit as if I had never seen it before. The answer was: Doug says you are to take this thing and fly it in the dark. Doug is infallible. Therefore, that is what you will do—and successfully at that. Engage brain function AUTO.

I taxied out, ran the engine up, looked up the approach path, and called the tower. Everything was normal on the takeoff roll. As soon as I was airborne, the instruments worked as they did when Doug was in the right seat. Climbing left turn on the gauges, glance back under the wing to make sure no one had crept up on me in the dark. The touch-and-go was a rough affair. While I was in the circuit the next time around, a de Havilland Dash 7 materialized out of the night and landed. I let myself float down the runway to stay above his wake. The landing that followed would have been creditable in daylight.

UZR could always be relied upon in a pinch. We put it into the hangar, shut everything up, and bade each other good night. Driving home, I was ready to fall asleep at the wheel. Five hours of night dual instruction is the legal minimum before a private pilot in Canada can fly solo at night. To make up for the nineteen hours it had taken me to solo in daylight, I had soloed at night after five hours and twenty minutes.

—16———————————

Things that Go Bump in the Night

People can say what they like about old pilots and bold pilots. It takes boldness to launch solo into the night sky. It was a dark, cold night, spitting rain from an invisible overcast. From the lit interior of the Flying Club, it looked remarkably unattractive. I wished that I had something more substantial than ZLG in which to take to the night sky—thicker armor against the brooding darkness.

As soon as the aircraft was fired up and taxiing, I began to merge with the night, a pair of wings and an all-seeing eye. Most of our waking time at night is spent in lit interiors. Even outside we like our world to be as brightly lit as possible for our daylight eyes to see. The night pilot is a creature of the night, accepting it rather than trying to beat it back. He sees not light, but lights. Each light is a signal, illuminating nothing but speaking volumes.

The orange lights of towns, laid out in perspective, show which way is up. As they become fewer, so must the pilot beware lest they deceive him. Where the lights end, often with a continuous faint line, there is water. A white light on the water is a ship. Two or three lights are a big ship. There is no ship to be seen, not even a dark ship on the dark water, just one white light. A red light is an obstruction, be it a mast or a hill. A cubic mile of rock is perhaps faintly seen as a greater darkness and one red light. A flashing light within the confusion of city lights is an airfield. A cluster of lights moving like fireflies in close formation, or a tiny galaxy gone astray, is another aircraft. There is no aircraft, only darkness between the lights, but the little formation slipping on its way with such determination shows that an aircraft is there.

As the pilot approaches the airfield, he runs the ground lights through his brain with computer-like iteration until they snap into place and there is the runway. Red approach lights, green threshold lights, white edge lights. And don't land between the blue lights because that is a taxiway and the owner of the little winking orange light won't like it if you land on top of him.

The pilot floats over the approach lights and down between the edge lights, which assure him of a runway waiting to caress him with its dark embrace. For there is no runway, only an abyss of darkness—and white edge lights. The lights come up beside him and he becomes aware of something ghosting beneath him in the glow of his wingtip lights. He feels for the runway with his wheels, now squeezing lift from the wings, now adding a hint of power.

Some people think that an aircraft lands at night by means of its landing lights. Big aircraft may do so, but in the light plane it is a snare and a delusion. The landing light spreads a pool of light just in front of the nose, which draws the pilot's attention. Before his first solo his instructor taught him to look far ahead and not peer at the runway in front of the nose, and here is the so-called landing light tempting him to do that very thing.

Landing at night by the runway lights is an exercise in pure perspective. Doug remarked that night flying teaches people to make better landings in daylight. I would say that I did not even know how to land an aircraft until I learned to fly at night.

One fine evening I arrived at the Flying Club expecting a quiet session of circuits and landings. To my surprise Doug was all fired up to take me on the navigation exercise that was part of the night flying course. It was a triangular route from Victoria to Abbotsford to Pitt Meadows and back to Victoria.

ZLG's propeller turned into a shimmering disc under the floodlights. I could not resist the feeling that it was an insubstantial craft in which to go voyaging about the night skies. The night was clear and calm, but moonless. We climbed eastbound over the islands, just visible as darker masses on the dark water. The lights on the mainland shore provided a vague horizon. We picked up the Morse identifier of the Bellingham VOR and set course by the needle.

The Fraser River floodplain was a carpet of lights from which individual towns stood out poorly. We told the Abbotsford tower controller that he was to have the dubious pleasure of our brief company. The airfield showed up as a flashing light in a field of darkness. To my surprise I had reduced speed and height to the correct proportions as the runway lights came into view. Other aircraft were in the circuit, and on final approach I wrestled with the wake of one that had landed just ahead of us.

We made a touch-and-go landing and headed for Pitt Meadows in a climbing turn. How strange is a touch-and-go landing at an airfield at night! You exchanged a brief litany by radio with a voice whose owner you could not see and would never meet. You saw lights in a certain pattern and of certain colors. You arranged those lights in a particular way and felt something solid under your wheels. You applied full power and the solid surface went away. Then you hunched over some instruments. A spinning wheel told you which way was up; a barometer told you how high you were; a little tube like a wetted finger held to the wind told you how much of the precious airspeed you had; a small chunk of metal faced toward its lord and master in the Arctic barrens far to the north of Kenora, Ontario, and you kept it shut up in a box and watched it to see which way you were heading. To the people at the airfield, you were a voice on the radio, some lights appearing out of the night, a chirrup of rubber on asphalt, a bellowing engine, and lights fading once more into the darkness from which they had briefly emerged.

On the way to Pitt Meadows, I carelessly allowed the aircraft to yaw off course. Consequently the airport appeared off our right wing instead of dead ahead where I had been looking for it. With a steep, full-flap approach to the narrow runway, Doug had to coach me through, and we landed with a bump before I realized that we were there. I made a mental note to avoid landing on a runway by night without having landed on it by day. I was also uncomfortably aware that night VFR without the benefit of radio navigation aids demanded more dead reckoning capability than I possessed.

Having landed, we taxied back past a row of sleeping airplanes. Doug showed me a real, live airplane trap which someone had cunningly laid out. The blue taxiway lights led straight on, but the taxiway took a dogleg to the right. If you were to keep on straight ahead, you would end up in a shallow ditch. We blew away into the night once more, leaving the local inhabitants to their circuits and landings.

You could fly to any airfield at night and there would be a couple of airplanes doing circuits and landings like fireflies around their nest (supposing that fireflies do nest). You could then go to another airfield twenty miles away and find a couple more airplanes buzzing around the patch while you, a wandering star, would appear out of the night, mingle with them briefly, and then vanish, unknown as before.

On the way back to Victoria, Doug communed with Vancouver Terminal, which could see us on radar. As a VFR aircraft with no transponder, we were of limited interest. Even so, the controller vectored us around the huge airliners which stabbed the night with their searchlight beams, and told us of other aircraft coming from Victoria. Airplanes were not the only flying creatures abroad that night. As we descended toward Victoria at 1,000 feet, a night bird flashed beneath us, illuminated by our landing light.

As the engine cooled and ticked behind the hangar, Doug and I sat discussing the reliability of engines as a factor in night flying. He reckoned that the chances of a properly maintained, properly run engine failing suddenly and without warning during a night flight were so slight as to be negligible.

It was now a matter of building up the necessary hours of solo flight to complete the requirements before Doug could sign my license "Night Flying." I asked permission to build up some of the time by flying to Abbotsford and back (Pitt Meadows was too hard to find). Something in the regulations, however, forbade anything except local flying on solo night training flights, so I had to be content with cruising the night skies over Victoria and Duncan. The quota was soon complete, and Doug duly endorsed my license.

—17—————————

Through the Clouds

In the spring of 1984, the Flying Club put on an "Advanced Private Pilot Course." The purpose was to introduce private VFR pilots to radio navigation, night flying, and the procedures for crossing the American border and flying in U.S. airspace. The course consisted of three evening lectures and two cross-country flights, one by day down south, and one by night within Canada. The day cross-country flight was an all-day affair to Boeing Field at Seattle, Olympia, Kelso, down the Columbia estuary to Astoria, up the coast to Hoquiam, and so home via the west coast of the Olympic Peninsula.

The course instructor was Tom Brenan. He struck a curious note by remarking, "We'll take an IFR-equipped aircraft—then we'll be sure of getting back if the weather turns sour." Was that the real difference between VFR and IFR? Certainty and uncertainty? Cross-country VFR was so filled with agonizing decisions, wasted planning, and canceled flights, so utterly dependent on the whims of the fickle weather that it was impossible to say with any certainty that any flight would be made and, if made, completed. This was especially true in winter. Using IFR, could a light plane pilot really fly where he wanted when he wanted? I was aware that light planes did fly IFR and that an instrument rating was a good and desirable thing but had no conception of how it worked in practice. I was about to find out.

Our crew assembled on a wet Sunday morning in March. Tom Brenan was our guide and leader. The three pupils on this flight were Sharon Neeves, Evelyn Greene, and myself. Sharon was an adventurous girl, an aerobatic pilot and a parachutist. Evelyn had won her wings the year before and had no night or instrument training. Our aircraft was the

Club's IFR-equipped Cessna 172, IJW.

I had to drag myself out of bed at 5:30 A.M. to reach the airport in time for a prompt eight o'clock departure. Steady rain fell from a high overcast. Wandering sunbeams lit the Gulf Islands to the southwest. It was by no means encouraging weather for a supposedly VFR flight.

With Sharon at the controls, we lifted off into a weeping sky, turgid with cloud and rain. We climbed to 5,500 feet over a gray sea flecked with foam. Clouds drifted by on either side of us and obscured some of the islands below. A man sitting at a radar screen on Whidbey Island in the murk to our left espied us with his magic eye. We exchanged cryptic and functional greetings with him and went our way.

The mouth of Puget Sound lay buried in cloud. Under the visual flight rules we had two alternatives. We could descend to low altitude and penetrate the rain and dim light between the cloud and the ground with the idea of navigating to Seattle visually and without hitting anything. In the alternative we could make the time-honored 180° turn, return to Victoria, and spend the day in other pursuits, having failed entirely to complete any part of our intended route. In that case I would have arisen bleary-eyed for nothing, and we would have achieved precisely nothing except to burn fuel and wear holes in our checkbooks.

The 180° turn in the face of foul weather or other problems is a life-saving maneuver. The pilot who has several in his logbook is regarded as a person of mature judgment and likely to live to a ripe old age. This does not alter the fact that it is an extraordinarily expensive way of achieving nothing. Smarter yet would be the pilot who had the prescience not to have taken off in the first place.

In this case Tom Brenan merely called Seattle Center on the radio and obtained an IFR clearance into Boeing Field. We continued above a rolling plain of cloud. Away south the Olympic Mountains, streaked with snow, rose out of one cloud deck only to conceal their peaks in a higher overcast which stretched overhead. Following radar vectors, we slid down toward the cloud. The crests of cloudy billows flashed past, and we drowned in an all-enveloping whiteness. There was no up, no down, no movement, only a stationary aircraft spreading its wings into the fog, its engine reverberating in our headphones.

It was the first time that any of the three pupils had been inside cloud in a small airplane, and the experience was one of immense elation. The VFR pilot is warned of the horrendous consequences of entering cloud, yet we were doing that very thing with impunity. Sharon flew imperturbably by instruments under Tom's watchful eye. I was as thrilled as a child on a seashore. Whether Evelyn fully appreciated the experience I have yet to discover.

The beams of the Boeing Field Instrument Landing System reached up into the cloud and tickled the needles on our instrument panel to life. We were flying an ILS approach. It seemed so simple. We broke out of cloud with downtown Seattle at our left elbows. I wondered if anyone down there realized what a special little airplane this was and what insight the occupants had so recently gained. The parallel runways of Boeing Field appeared through the falling rain, and we were on the ground not long afterward, deplaning into the fresh, rain-scented air.

We sauntered into the U.S. Customs office as if we had just disembarked from a small boat—which, in a sense, we had. The official accepted that we were innocent people bent on minding our own business. How much better was this than standing in front of an airline ticket desk for an hour and then being treated as a dangerous criminal by a variety of officious persons. At the Flight Service Station we checked the weather. The talk was of fronts and depressions, but the main idea was clouds and rain in all directions. We filed an IFR flight plan to Olympia. Galvin's Flight Service provided coffee free for the drinking, of which we made good use while the air traffic control computer chewed on our flight plan.

We huddled under IJW's wing in the rain, then climbed in, and took off. Soon we were in cloud once more. Radar vectors sent us over the top of Seattle-Tacoma airport, which we saw through a gap in the clouds. South of Seattle the clouds were cumulus. We approached them from the side, gulped, and plunged in. We were in cloud most of the time, but, during brief periods in clear air, we caught glimpses of an intricate coastline and a maze of channels and forested islands. Seattle Center vectored us to the Olympia ILS, but, soon after finding it, we broke out of cloud. Although the airfield was not immediately visible, it was simple enough to find our way there.

We taxied up to Pearson's Flying Service and let the line boy fill our tanks. Pearson's had an ancient Chev for the use of customers, and we drove into town for a bite to eat, which, in the American style, was most ample.

In the early afternoon we took off again with Evelyn at the helm. This time we were determined to remain VFR, which turned out to be more easily said than done. Our route followed the interstate highway to Kelso, 55 miles away. The cloud was barely 1,000 feet above a rainwashed landscape of rectangular fields and patches of forest. At one point we popped up over a cloud and then ducked down through a hole again to find that the highway had sneaked off to one side so that we almost lost it.

The terrain funneled us down into a narrowing valley with stuffed clouds on either side. (The expression "a stuffed cloud" means cloud with hilltops concealed in it.) We crept along at reduced power with 10° of flap extended. We had to consider turning back. After some time and suspense the valley opened out and the town of Kelso came into sight. We landed on a runway gleaming in the rain. From talking to other pilots in the Windsock Cafe, we learned that the weather between Kelso and Olympia was exactly on the margins of VFR. Some pilots were getting through; others were turning back. I could not help speculating how it would be to be stuck in Kelso on a wet Sunday afternoon, restricted to VFR, with a job to get back to on Monday morning. Telephoning the boss and saying you will be absent because you went flying and got weathered in is an explanation that sounds better in theory than in practice, especially when alternative employment is not plentiful.

After deciding to press on at least as far as Astoria (*Per Ardua ad Astoria*), we lifted off over the sawmills and lumber yards beside the Columbia River, which meandered down a valley five miles wide. The hills to the north and south rose into the cloud which roofed the valley at 2,000 feet. The Portland Flight Service Station radio operator told us that the Hoquiam weather was entirely opaque. Over Astoria we filed an IFR flight plan by radio and turned north. The sullen waters of the Pacific faded into the mist.

Once more we unrolled the magic carpet of IFR and went on our way, where a restriction to VFR would have left us hemmed in by deadly mists and fogs. On instructions from Seattle Center, we climbed to 6,000 feet. Milk-white masses of fog towered up ahead, obscuring the coast. Quite soon we were into the stuff. Tom asked Evelyn if she had had any instrument training. "Yes," she replied, "right now!" From time to time we looked down chasms in the cloud to the very bottom of the sky, where the Pacific roiled and foamed along the sandspits of the Washington coast. For the most part we droned on through the whiteness. Spongy white ice appeared on the wheels and wing struts and on the leading edges of the wings. We asked for a lower altitude and were assigned 5,000 feet, where the ice melted off.

Any aircraft flying in cloud where the air temperature is between roughly +2°C and -12°C can accumulate ice on the leading edges of the wings, propeller blades, and fuselage. Ice destroys the aerodynamic qualities of whatever it forms on, with the ultimate result that the aircraft will no longer fly. Large aircraft (from light twins upward) have equipment to dislodge ice or prevent it from forming. Small aircraft have none. The probability of ice accretion can be forecast from a knowledge of temperatures aloft. In our case the freezing level was forecast to be at 5,000 feet, and we were not surprised to pick up ice at 6,000.

Ice is one of the factors that restrict the use of small aircraft under IFR, especially in winter. There are occasions when all aircraft are grounded, no matter how large, how powerful, and how sophisticated. As likely as not, ice will be one of the factors. The light plane pilot must accept, therefore, that even with IFR capability certain weather and certain routes may be unflyable.

As we approached Hoquiam, it became apparent from the radio chatter that every aircraft on the Pacific coast was converging on the place, including a Cherokee pilot who confessed that he had misread his instruments and was unsure of his position. Even though it was a small local airport, Hoquiam had a published instrument approach. All of a sudden we found a hole in the cloud barely half a mile across, directly over the Hoquiam VOR, whose bright orange and white antenna house we could see on a small mud island below.

Tom canceled our IFR flight plan, and down we went in a steep spiral with the wind rumbling in our flaps. We leveled out in poor visibility only 700 feet above the mudbanks and sandspits of the Chehalis estuary. We flew slowly along a finger of land, looking for the Sunny Shores airstrip. "Foggy Shores" would have been a more accurate description at the time. The runway was a narrow strip of asphalt in the middle of a golf course. One end was a branch off the village main street. We landed in a strong crosswind.

The airstrip was run by a pleasant couple with whom we chatted as we figured out what to do next. It was my turn to fly the final leg of our journey. I was eager to discover IFR firsthand, and it was the most practical, if not the only, way to return to Victoria. There was no point in continuing up the coast as planned. Visibility was minimal in fog. Inland toward Seattle the land was generally lower than 1,000 feet, although certainly rising to nearly 500 feet. We had no means of finding out how much clear air, if any, existed between the cloud and the ground. Rain and fog might develop as we flew. Visual flight at low altitude might be possible, but then, too, it might not. In any case, it would be a difficult and possibly a dangerous operation.

Tom filed an IFR flight plan by telephone and, after waiting for it to sink in among the authorities, we boarded the aircraft. Tom handled the takeoff because the runway was narrow and the crosswind strong. A private pilot license is no guarantee of immediate proficiency, and anyone who thinks it is can fly himself into bad trouble. The private pilot flight test merely assures the authorities that the pilot can operate the aircraft safely in reasonable conditions. Flying is hedged about with countless regulations, which are by their nature exact, yet the sky and the individual's adaptation to flight are filled with inexactitudes within which the pilot must act according to his judgment.

We lifted off and turned out to sea, climbing at full throttle. Tom passed control of the aircraft to me. The fog closed in about us. We found the 046° radial from the Hoquiam VOR and continued our climb. Seattle Center assigned us 6,000 feet. Once more we started to collect ice and had to ask for 5,000 feet. Even a little ice immediately reduced our speed by 10 knots. The ice melted slowly, and we flew on inside the cloud for 40 miles. Through a gap we caught a glimpse of an airfield, which gave us direct confirmation of our whereabouts.

As we approached Seattle, the radar controller gave us a vector northward to take us some 20 miles west of the city. We emerged into a patch of clear sky, perhaps 30 miles across, under a high overcast. The controller was talking to other unseen aircraft around Seattle, but we went our way without further conversation, other than to arrange a climb to 6,000 feet in order to overtop the next cloud bank which rolled toward us, hiding the rain-soaked land. Soon it was time to begin our descent toward Victoria, and we sank once more down through the cloud.

We broke out of cloud at 4,000 feet over the Straits of Juan de Fuca, I had been eagerly anticipating an instrument approach into Victoria, but I found that I was unexpectedly tired and, because the airport was clear of cloud, we canceled our IFR flight plan. Tom told me to land straight in on runway 31. I could not make out why we were going so fast, even with full flaps, until I realized that we were landing in a cross-tailwind. Cross-tailwinds seldom make for good landings.

We taxied in to the Customs office as the airfield lights came on. The long-suffering girl behind the desk bore our flippant remarks with good grace without throwing us all into jail, and we headed for the Flying Club. It was a bone-weary and ravenous crew who went their separate ways to dream of IJW's voice booming in their headphones and the surreal beauty of pearl-gray cloudscapes unrolling beneath their wings. I was hooked on IFR from that day.

—18

Interlude: Gone Flying

"Mr. Jones? I'm afraid he's not here right now. He's gone flying."

"How do you mean, 'gone flying'?"

"Flying—like—airplanes? He flies airplanes. In fact he's probably flying one right now."

"How long will this 'flying' go on?"

"He should be back in an hour or two."

"No, I mean, how long does he intend to continue this 'flying'?"

"It could well be a lifelong affair."

"Oh. Anyway, where could I get hold of him?"

"You could try the flying club."

❊ ❊ ❊

"Good morning, this is the flying club. . . . Mr. Jones? Let me see. . . . He's flying right now. . . . He should be back in an hour. . . . If it's really urgent, you might try the control tower, but I doubt if they'll be able to get ahold of him."

❊ ❊ ❊

"Good morning, this is the control tower. . . . No sir, we have no knowledge of the pilot's name unless you can give me the aircraft type and registration. . . . A flying club aircraft? Just a minute. . . . We believe there are two flying club aircraft flying at this time, but they both cleared this frequency some time ago. . . . Good day, sir."

❊ ❊ ❊

Mr. Jones is a busy man and seldom far from a telephone.

"Mr. Jones, there's a council meeting this evening."

"Mr. Jones, will you mend my lawnmower like you did last time, please?"

"Mr. Jones, will you help us with the ways and means committee? Good. There's a meeting at nine o'clock on Saturday morning."

"Mr. Jones, there's a Mr. Smith to see you from Revco."

"Mr. Jones, do you have that report that's due in to the Board tomorrow?"

"Mr. Jones, it's Swash and Hardbuckle on the line. They want to talk to you about the lease."

But today, right now, Mr. Jones has gone. Gone flying.

※ ※ ※

Just recently Mr. Jones won his wings as a private pilot. Before that he was too busy practicing to do much flying. Run that by me again!? I said, "He was too busy practicing maneuvers for the flight test to do much flying." Let me explain. The flight test required that he perform certain maneuvers to certain standards. It never required him to fly.

Of course it required him to take control of an aircraft and cause it to fly. Being a conscientious person, he practiced the evolutions he was told to practice until he could perform them to the required standards of accuracy as set forth in *Transport Canada Flight Test Guide TP2655E Private and Commercial Licences: Aeroplane Eighth Edition June 1980*. The demands of flight training weighed heavily on him, his own fears, his responsibility for an expensive and delicate piece of equipment, his realization of his own limited capacity and of the lethal dangers which stalked through the jungles of his ignorance.

He manipulated the controls as he had been taught. If he was told to move a control, he moved it. If he was told to feel a control pressure, he felt it. If he was told to perceive a phenomenon, he perceived it. If he was told to beware of certain situations, he did so. Accordingly he caused the perspectives of the world to unravel in certain ways, needles on the cockpit instruments to point to prescribed numbers, and the aircraft to travel to and from specified locations expeditiously. Secretly he thought he was quite a good pilot because he had an orderly mind and could do these things with a fair degree of accuracy.

Eventually the flight test examiner shook his hand and said, "Well done." Everyone else shook his hand and said, "Well done." The marks on the scoresheet showed that this was indeed so. But the flight test never required him to fly because it could not take his lid off and look inside to see if he was flying.

Then he read a book with an obvious title, written by a man with a German name about a block and a half long such that even persons acting in good faith had arguments about how to pronounce it. He began to understand that an airplane flew. When cavemen threw rocks at each other, the rocks traveled through the air but they did not fly. When the first Chinaman lit the first touch paper on the first rocket (or, shall we say, the first rocket to behave as intended), it also traveled through the air but it did not fly. The hot air balloons and the dirigibles and the blimps all traveled through the air or floated in it like clouds, but they never flew. But then a variety of late Victorians made things with wings which actually flew, and often killed themselves in the process. Mr. Jones began to realize that even a Boeing 747, shaking the ground with its thunder, was not propelled by thrust like a rocket; it did not follow a trajectory like an artillery shell. It flew. It rested the whole of its vast bulk on thin air.

It was a cold weekday morning in late autumn. Mr. Jones inspected the little airplane and looked up at the high overcast. The air was still; there were few people about. The flying club did not do much business on cold weekday mornings in late autumn. He climbed in, strapped himself to the stiff plastic of the cold seat, and snapped the door shut. Gradually the airplane came to life under his fingers. Voices spoke to each other on the radio; the engine rumbled to itself; warmth began to waft through the hot air vent. At length they stood ready beside the runway, looking up the approach path. The voice from the control tower said that they could fly.

They were picking up speed along the runway when a curious thing happened, as it has happened for every pilot who ever took off in any airplane ever built. The aircraft began to fly. It did not fly all at once; it *began* to fly. The control surfaces were no longer ineffectual flippers. They became alive, springy. The magic lift force blossomed around the wings, and quite soon there was so much that the aircraft floated away from the ground. It was transformed from an ungainly and pointless structure burdened with awkward and fragile members into a creature held in a web of mysterious forces, a creature that flew. Mr. Jones felt that this was good air to fly in—cold, dense, and still, like clear syrup.

Mr. Jones looked down from a height at the brown land etched with blown snow. He looked out at the undersides of the wings and saw the air flowing beneath them, producing the magic force called lift. He looked back over the tail and felt the little airplane flying. He looked about the inside of the tiny cabin, put his feet on the floor, and folded his hands while the aircraft flew on brainlessly by itself. He was a man sitting in an aircraft.

He placed his toes on the rudder pedals, took the yoke in his left hand and the throttle in his right, and went into a steep turn. He was no longer a man sitting in an aircraft; he was the aircraft. Its wings were his wings; his mind was its mind. He looked down at a farmyard turning beneath his wingtip, rolled level, and few on. Hand in hand, aircraft and pilot walked through the gray halls of cold air. Their footfalls rang in the brooding silence of the vast winter sky. Mr. Jones was flying.

Of course there was no valid reason for not doing spins.

"Why do you want to do spins?"

"I don't. The view is fine right side up."

"Then why do them? Or are you chicken?"

"No, I'm not chicken. I just don't feel like spins right now."

"If you walk away from this flight without doing spins, it'll prove you're chicken."

Mr. Jones wiped his hands on the knees of his trousers. He and the aircraft took stock of each other momentarily, like dancing partners. At Mr. Jones's bidding the aircraft capsized into the mad, rolling, vertiginous fall so innocently called a spin. The fear bit him, but he threw it from him and it had no power over him. He looked up with detachment at the brown earth gyrating overhead. Wail of the stall warning, fluttering of the slowly turning propeller, shuddering and creaking of the aircraft, revolving ground, one turn, aircraft lifts its nose and looks around, pitches down again, two turns, tramp opposite rudder, unstall the wings, let it fly, pull a couple of g's or the airspeed will go into the yellow arc, zoom into a climb, push forward and go weightless over the top. Earth and sky resumed their normal positions. Mr. Jones was flying.

They turned back toward the airport. Sighing, they sank down through the cold sky like the dead leaves riding the autumn wind. The aircraft spoke to the control tower with Mr. Jones's voice. They floated down final approach, the propeller windmilling slowly, the engine purring and muttering. They flared out just above the hard, black runway, floated briefly, and touched lightly. The wings gave up their lift; the controls slackened; the aircraft was once more a clumsy and fragile structure trundling along the ground.

Mr. Jones had gone flying.

19

That First Hundred Hours

Bob Sherman and I were doing some hangar flying in Molly's Coffee Shop one day when the conversation turned to "How I survived my first hundred hours." The answers we agreed on were: (a) don't know, (b) luck, (c) we flew only in fine weather, (d) we didn't wander far afield, (e) we were extremely cautious. We both looked back, appalled at how little we had known.

I had sworn that I would not carry passengers until I had amassed 100 hours of flight time, but even so, I discovered in a hurry that if people, in blissful ignorance, entrusted their lives to my hot-and-stickies, I became tense and distracted from the primary job of flying the airplane. Consequently, they did not enjoy the ride any more than I did.

By himself, or with a pilot friend, a newly licensed pilot can look at the sky, feel the wind, and decide whether to go. The pilot friend can be relied upon to make himself useful and not to flap his yap at inopportune moments such as on final approach. As soon as non-pilot passengers enter the scene, the pressure is on to produce results. Passengers themselves may be nervous and tend to divert the pilot's attention from the task at hand, which demands his total concentration. You will not often see passengers in the cockpit of an airliner, and certainly not during departure or arrival. This distraction can lead to a common accident scenario in which a brand-new licensed pilot takes passengers in a rented aircraft and promptly rolls it up in a ball on takeoff or landing. Nothing untoward happened on my first passenger-carrying flight, but months passed before I took passengers again.

Toward the end of May, the evenings lengthened and the weather calmed. I sidled up to Doug one day, drew a deep breath, and asked if he would teach me aerobatics. In the quiet of the evening, we took off in the Cessna 150 Aerobat, IDS, with the occupant of the left seat wondering what he had let himself in for. Doug had not only flown aerobatics in Mustangs and Harvards and Vampires and T-33s and Sabres; he had not only taught aerobatics; he had led Air Force formation aerobatic teams. Whether military, bush, airline, or instruction, Doug had spent more time on any one aspect of flying than most private pilots stack up in a lifetime.

Over the practice area the normally bucolic IDS bellowed happily through chandelles and lazy eights. The altimeter wound and unwound like a demented clock. The vertical speed needle occupied parts of the dial which I had never previously noticed. I instantly developed a new confidence in the flying propensities of the aircraft and my ability to control them.

A hammerhead—now there's something different! We push over into a shallow dive. The slipstream becomes a mass of hissing snakes and whistling gremlins. At 105 knots the controls are firm to the touch. A gentle backward pressure on the yoke squeezes us into our seats as the aircraft hauls up into a vertical climb. We ease in full throttle, and there is nothing but sky. I wonder if we will reach that little cloud. I think not. A Cessna 150 does not stay in a vertical climb for long, and we are rapidly losing airspeed. As the airspeed needle slides back past 65 knots, we push in full rudder and ease off the yoke pressure to prevent ourselves from going upside down. Quick! Push forward to keep us vertical, and we are weightless with the engine lugging and the propeller thrashing as the aircraft slowly cartwheels into a vertical dive. Power OFF! That field ahead is so very green, and there are cows in it. The airspeed indicator has woken up after registering nothing at all. We coax the aircraft into level flight—and that's a hammerhead.

With the next lesson came precision spins. In a precision spin the pilot resumes normal flight after an exact number of turns or fractions of turns. No two individual aircraft spin alike. Indeed, unless the spin entries are the same, no two spins are exactly alike. Doug showed me how to use a road or some other linear feature on the ground for alignment. A Cessna 150 winds up into a spin during the first three turns. Therefore, the lead time on the controls needed to stop the spin on a predetermined heading depends on the number of turns contemplated to begin with. There was no denying that spins still frightened me, but the precision spin was a way out of it—to have such total control over the aircraft that I could spin and stop spinning exactly at will.

At this point my Category 1 medical certificate came through. I turned to the somewhat less interesting pursuit of a commercial license.

Harvey Taggart won his private license in the spring, and we soon started flying together. We caused plenty of laughter, both to ourselves and to other people, with our elaborate preparations to get off the ground and with our almost impossibly bad luck with the weather, but it seemed to work.

At Victoria the new private pilot was hemmed in by uninhabited mountain country to the north and west and by the American border to the south. East were the Straits of Georgia and the lower Fraser Valley, which was only some 50 miles long. Part of that was the Vancouver control zone, where we risked being ingested by Boeing 747s and were therefore not entirely welcome. We were slow to penetrate these barriers. Our idea of VFR weather was blue sky with light winds and no more than a cumulus or two over the hills and islands. It was fun, nevertheless, and more extensive travels would keep until later.

As the evenings drew out and darkness came later, it became easy to forget about night flying, and I had to make an effort to retain my still meager proficiency. One fine evening I floated into the golden sky in IJW and climbed southwestward over the lakes and forests of the Victoria watershed where I worked. From 4,000 feet I could see across the Strait of Juan de Fuca to the snow-capped Olympic Mountains. To the west the jungly hills of the island stretched range upon gray-black range to the flame-yellow horizon. Southeast the lights of Victoria spangled the dusk. Around the eastern arc of the horizon, the lights of the mainland shone through the rising night.

The seaward end of the East Sooke Peninsula was wreathed in the merest breath of low cloud. To the airman, as to no one else, is revealed the infinite subtlety of the sky. Why call it meteorology or burden it with long and dusty names? It is the sky itself. The mariner and the weatherman observe it only from below. To them the sky is a dome from which come rain and sunshine, heat and cold. Only the airman voyages within it and feels its limitless capacity for change. He knows its foulest moods, of high winds, thunderstorms, and ice-laden clouds, and cowers on the ground. He knows, too, its utter gentleness. Climbing through the warm dusk, he feels a shivering in his wings. Looking about him for the reason, he sees the knife edge of a veil of haze marking a temperature inversion. Looking down, he sees a fluff of mist breaking over a coast. Slow-drifting air over the water breathes on the shoreline. The land disturbs the delicate balance of temperature and humidity; water vapor

condenses. The air moves on; the water droplets evaporate, a garland
of cloud ever forming, ever vanishing along a rocky shore.

We circled slowly over my home in Sooke. Darkness was slow in
coming this high summer evening. The light lingered in the northwestern
sky even as a huge yellow moon sailed up in the east to take its place.
The little airplane roamed over Metchosin, feeling with its antennae the
rays from the radio beacons which criss-crossed the sky, picking one
up, savoring it, following it for a while, and leaving it for another.

Back at the airport the runway was clearly visible under the full
moon. Landing was surprisingly difficult, with interesting and by no
means desirable results. Flaring out in the glare of a Hercules's landing
lights, I slapped the aircraft onto the ground hard and flat and bounced
along the runway. The next attempt was worse; I hoped no one was
looking. At my third attempt I bounced again. I sat tight and waited.
After a few split seconds it dawned on me that I must have bounced
several feet into the air (you cannot see much at night). Unless I took
steps, and pretty quick ones, the aircraft would fall to the ground with
a gear-wrecking smash. I opened the throttle to break the fall, but still
we did not touch down. Because we were still safely airborne, I applied
the rest of the available power and we left the ground somewhere
beneath us. For the first time in solo flight, I was assailed by the thought:
"I am up here. The ground is down there. Somehow I have to get *there*
from *here,* and I'm not sure I know how."

Now concentrate, fool, it's only sloppy flying. You know what to
do, so do it! Call the tower on the downwind leg of the circuit—cleared
for a touch-and-go. There are the green lights at the touchdown end of
the runway. Turn your head full left. Don't turn yet. Wait for it. Head
full left, eyes full left, looking at the green threshold lights. Carburetor
heat hot, power 1,200 rpm. Go onto the instruments because the left
wing will hide the ground lights in the turn. Thirty-degree-banked
descending left turn onto a heading of 354°. Trim for 70 knots. Level
the wings, extend 10° of flap, airspeed 65 knots. Runway in sight.
Continue on base leg and intercept the runway centerline. Fifteen-
degree-banked turn onto final approach. Jockey the power a little. Make
it a stable approach at 65 knots aimed just beyond the threshold lights.
Slide in over the threshold. Don't mess around; just sit tight. Look at the
edge lights, not the runway. There's the runway ghosting by underneath.
Bring the nose up so you can only just see the lights at the far end. Hold
the nose up and let the aircraft settle until it touches—screech-screech
. . . screech. Power off. That's better. Carb heat cold, flaps up,

flashglance to see that they are retracting, shot of nose-up trim, full throttle. Do it again and you can call it quits.

I had finished flying one velvet calm night. No one was about, and I was free to sit in the aircraft, listening to the gyroscopes running down and the engine ticking, and to dream dreams. A bizjet landed with a soft howl and flashing strobes. It taxied in past the flight line and stopped in front of the tower, only the auxiliary power unit running with a subdued shriek. A wine-red limousine came out of the shadows and drew up to the aircraft. The chauffeur opened the car door. From within the aircraft a door opened and steps unfolded. The personage alighted and was spirited away in the limousine. The aircraft shut itself up again. The deeper note of the engines came up under that of the auxiliary power unit, and soon their siren howl propelled the pinball strobes into the night sky. Climbing at full throttle toward the northeast, the winking strobes were lost among the stars.

I stretched, opened the door, tied the airplane down, put chocks under the wheels, made sure the journey log was filled in, walked around it once, whispered: "Good night, airplane," and walked quietly away.

—20————————————————

The Commercial Ticket

There is a difficult period in the life of the civilian pilot. It is generally recognized as beginning when he wins his wings and gradually fading out when he has accumulated some 250–300 flying hours. Of the fatal accidents involving single-engined landplanes, 40% happen to private pilots with fewer than 300 hours of flying time. It could well be that a significant proportion of the total flying time of single-engined landplanes is flown by low-time private pilots, but the statistic is a shocker. There is nothing magic about 300 hours. It just means that by that time the pilot has probably acquired enough savvy to keep himself out of trouble. The time in between is the time to be earning additions to the license.

In the course of learning to fly, I had become aware of a qualification called a commercial pilot license. The Canadian requirements as to flying time put it somewhere within my reach and were less than those for the instrument rating. It was difficult to discover what the training consisted of, not least because the Transport Canada syllabus was itself vague. The gist of the answers to my questions was that both the flight training and the groundschool imparted a deeper understanding than did the private pilot course. About half of the flying time consisted of instrument flying. My long-term objective was to obtain an instrument rating and, although this training did not add up to one, it was a useful start.

I won my private pilot wings with 62 hours of flight time of which 27 were as pilot-in-command (solo). Regardless of the progress of my training, the instrument rating could not be issued until I had 150 hours as pilot-in-command. A private pilot whose flying is restricted to spare evenings and weekends flies a great deal if he marks up 100 hours in a year. After all, that represents two hours a week, fifty weeks a year. An hour or two on the ground can be added to the air time of every flying expedition. This is without mentioning that 100 hours cost $5,000 or more in aircraft rentals. There is therefore a gap of 12 to 18 months, in terms of flying time, from the private license to the minimum flight time required for the instrument rating. I decided to fill this gap with the pursuit of a commercial license. Besides this, the employment scene was not a bright one; my tunneling job was only for the duration of the project. A commercial pilot license would be a useful card up my sleeve.

When a student pilot first learns to fly, he chalks up 10 to 20 hours of dual instruction, then his instructor pats him on the back and tells him to fly himself around the patch. Thereafter he is free to take off and fly by himself in visual conditions. He is not free to do so in instrument conditions until he has 150 hours as pilot-in-command and has passed the IFR flight test. Where there are bear tracks, there is likely a bear. Flying "blind" through cloud is obviously not a simple process. There are several stages in learning to do so.

The most basic instrument flying skill is the ability to retain control of the aircraft by instruments alone, which is taught for the night endorsement. Next comes the ability to fly exact headings, altitudes, and airspeeds, and to deduce the aircraft's position by means of radio beacon receivers in the aircraft. These two skills are required for the commercial license. The next two steps are specific to the training for the instrument rating. The first is to learn instrument approaches, which are set-piece procedures combining precise instrument flying and radio navigation. The second consists of learning the enroute procedures, which brings everything together and adds communication with air traffic controllers.

Instrument flying is taught in clear skies by day or by night using the moderately effective method of placing a hood over the pupil's brow, which hides the outside world. Sunlight and glimpses outside (even accidental ones) provide a good many hints as to which way is up, and there is not the knowledge of total dependence on the instruments, which is the case when flying in cloud. However, no aircraft is allowed to enter cloud unless on an IFR flight plan or clearance, and therefore the instrument trainee cannot learn in real instrument conditions until the later stages of his training. Quite often we could not fly instrument dual because the weather was IFR.

Said Doug, as we taxied out to the run-up pad beside the runway:

"You already know how to fly on the instruments. We'll start off with some of the high-intensity stuff." And we did. Doug taxied IMH out onto the runway and gave me control of the aircraft for an instrument takeoff. This exercise is nothing less than charging along the runway blind and taking off entirely by instruments. The instructor is looking out at the surroundings. A wide runway and no crosswind are necessary precautions.

We flew circuits and overshoots. We took each approach to 100 feet above ground and then poured on the power and kept going. Doug kept a sharp lookout for obstacles and other aircraft, and gave me headings and altitudes to fly, because at this stage I was not in a position to use the radio approach aids even if the aircraft had been equipped to receive them. After forty-five minutes around the circuit, our final approach was the real thing. Doug flared the aircraft out, and we touched down. "*Now* you can take the hood off," said he. I stared at the scenery as if I had landed from the moon.

It is a long step from merely keeping the aircraft under control by instruments to flying exact headings and altitudes. A summer evening would see Doug and me taking off in a Cessna 152 for instrument dual. For the most part I saw nothing outside the aircraft from the moment we were ready for takeoff until we were 300 feet above ground on final approach to land. I could not but feel that it was a strange way to spend the summer. When the weather was grungy, we were not allowed to fly in real instrument conditions, yet when the sky was clear way on up into space, on went the hood and I was stuck with herding needles around the instrument dials. I might as well have stayed on the ground. Unfortunately, only a small percentage of the training can be done in a simulator because nothing can simulate the whims of a small airplane without costing as much as a fleet of them.

The instrument pilot must closely control altitude and heading simultaneously. Therefore, as soon as the trainee has learned to control them separately, he must combine them. In a Cessna 152 our standard rate of climb was 700 feet per minute; of descent, 500 feet per minute; of turn, 3° per second. When the instructor sets up a maneuver involving a turning climb or descent between specified headings and altitudes, he can arrange it so that the pupil must straighten out before, after, or at the same time as leveling off at the new altitude. Demands for precision soon follow. For brief periods my brain would turn itself off in disgust while the altimeter needles and direction indicator (the gyroscopic compass) went around and around however seemed good to them. If the gray matter turned itself on again before the assigned heading or altitude came up, well and fine. If not, we overshot the mark. Fortunately it was not a serious issue at that point. The sky is a big place, and we gave ourselves plenty of elbow room (at least I think we did).

Training in unusual (a.k.a. absurd, insane) attitudes was also on the agenda, as was "partial panel" simulating a failure of the two main gyroscopic instruments: the attitude indicator and the direction indicator. There were recoveries on partial panel from what felt like the tops of hammerheads, from spiral dives, from straight-ahead stalls, power on and power off, and from two-turn spins entered from full-power climbing turns. Doug had maneuvers up his sleeve to assist in the process. What they were he never said. I never asked.

"Partial panel" was another stage in the training. The six basic instruments have three separate power sources. One is air pressure; the vents can ice up or become accidentally blocked. Another is a DC electric motor driving a gyroscope, which can fail. The third is the suction pump driving two gyroscopes, which can also fail. The last of these is the most common, and it takes out the attitude indicator and direction indicator at the same time. But Doug had other ideas besides. No pupil of his was going to be let loose in clouds without a shrewd idea of what to do if everything were to pack up one after another. Doug was not prepared to bet anyone's life on the supposition that equipment cannot fail. He had known many of the backwaters of the aviation business and knew whereof he spoke.

As we cruised the sky above Duncan on "solid instruments" in a cloudless sky, Doug disgorged an apparently endless supply of rubber suction discs from his pockets to cover the instruments. First he covered the attitude and direction indicators to simulate a vacuum pump failure and consequent running down of the gyroscopes, leaving "needle, ball, and airspeed"—which is all the first instrument pilots had.

"Your static vent iced up," said Doug. Out came three more suction discs to cover the altimeter, airspeed indicator, and vertical speed indicator. I turned up the gain control on my brain by several decibels. The average pilot has a backup airspeed indicator sticking out each side of his head and in such a situation they become remarkably sensitive. Turns had to be timed rate-one turns because of the various crazy things the magnetic compass does in a turn. If a rate-one turn is a change of heading of 3° per second, which way do you turn, and for how long to turn from 050° to 290°? Easy enough to calculate when sitting on the ground, but not so easy under the hood.

"Now descend a thousand feet." A power reduction of 500 rpm as read on the tachometer would give a 500-feet-per-minute descent, which, if continued for two minutes, would give a descent of 1,000 feet (and possibly even an emergence into clear air). Doug pulled another sticker from his pocket: "Your DC gyro just packed up." That left me sneaking glances at the magnetic compass on the windshield, trying not to notice the real horizon outside. We wobbled along for a while.

Doug pulled the disc off the altimeter. "Now how would you know that you were in a turn with no directional indication at all?" That presupposed the destruction or failure of the magnetic compass, the attitude indicator and direction indicator, and the turn coordinator (needle and ball), which runs off the battery even if the engine fails. The answer was that at a constant trim and power setting the aircraft would lose height if the wings were not level. How the pilot was supposed to know which way he was turning, and so avoid making it worse, I thought it impolitic to ask at that point.

Finally Doug took off all the discs, causing me to look with disdain at so many redundant instruments—precisely the purpose of the lesson. This had not only been "partial panel"; it had been instrument flying without instruments. Doug told me to take off the hood and admire the view. Now it was my turn: "Doug, if it's OK with you, I'll put it back on. I need the practice." The next time I saw outside, we were 200 feet above ground on final approach. Because we had about fifteen seconds to touchdown, there was nothing but to sit back and land.

I sauntered into the office behind Doug, nonchalantly swinging the hood from my forefinger so everybody could take note and be duly impressed. Jeremy Rimmer had also been flying.

"What have you guys been up to?" he asked.

"Oh, just partial panel," I replied.

"What instruments did he cover up?"

Now that was getting technical. I scratched my head, trying to remember how many instruments the bird had anyway.

"Well, kind of, just about all of them."

"Which ones did he leave in then?"

Jeremy, you ask too many questions.

"Well, there was a compass. And a clock. And that was about it."

It was Jeremy's turn to do some head-scratching.

Doug put in: "I hoped he'd go into a spin or a spiral dive or something, but he didn't. No fun at all."

—21

Style

With the impatience of the novice, I began to feel that the words "Basic Instrument Flying" were appearing in the "Remarks" column of my logbook with monotonous regularity, with only brief excursions into VORs, NDBs, holding patterns, and the like. I began to wonder what the future held in store.

Doug was a man of sphinx-like reticence. He said that he would be away briefly, but when I telephoned to arrange the next lesson, I discovered that he had retired. Despite being a flying instructor and, as such, in contact with a wide variety of people, Doug was a shy, private man. Many things were his business and no one else's. He saw and knew many things which he kept to himself. I never heard him utter a word which was not worth hearing. I often hung around, just listening. If he was capable of meanness, self-seeking, or dishonesty, it will be news to me. He was utterly sensitive to the most subtle nuances of wind and weather. Those who took his instruction to heart would, above all, absorb an attitude toward the whole business of flying which would always protect them—a way of flight. If I were to tell you that Doug MacColl taught me to fly, you would see a distant gaze of reminiscence in my eyes and a slow smile spreading. Around the Flying Club Doug was sadly missed.

Doug's retirement left me with the need to find another instructor. My three aims were to complete the training for my commercial license, to obtain an instrument rating, and to learn something of aerobatics.

The purpose of holding a private pilot license is to fly small airplanes, either as a form of recreation with occasional travel or as an achievement in itself. That suffices. In the more advanced areas of flight, the achievements of the private license are taken for granted.

Flying becomes more serious and the motivation necessarily more intense. The pilot is seeking to promote himself from the ranks of Sunday-afternoon flyers. A different style of instruction is needed.

A commercial license entitles the pilot ultimately to fly paying passengers who entrust their lives to his skill and judgment and rely on him to deliver them punctually to a destination, using an expensive aircraft to make a profit for its owner. An instrument rating allows him to fly complex routings and maneuvers blind in cloud by sole reference to the aircraft's flight instruments and navigation radios. Aerobatics involve the pilot in violent, stressful, and disorientating maneuvers. In all three cases the penalties for incompetence are extreme. It follows that a ceaseless demand for perfection and a frank, if brutal (although not necessarily cruel, personal, or sarcastic), exposition of the trainee's deficiencies is not only appropriate but essential: "If you can't stand the heat, stay out of the kitchen." This way of thought and mode of instruction is not equally appropriate to private pilot training and probably has driven away many people who otherwise would be flying happily and competently today.

For this reason I sought out, by reputation, the most demanding and outspoken instructor I could find—a man named Jack Kaiser. Jack had been flying Lancasters over Germany while his contemporaries were still at school. He had gone on to fly everything from four-engined transports to Starfighters, and had been in command of Royal Canadian Air Force flight training. Since retiring from the Air Force, he had been closely associated with the Victoria Flying Club in managerial and instructional capacities. He also held a test pilot rating. He had published two books: *How To Fly: Cessna 150* and *How To Fly: Instruments*.

My initial contact was not too encouraging. I had booked a lesson with him while he was still on vacation, without having discussed the idea with him first, perhaps an unwise move. I had diligently preflighted ZLG and had just finished fueling it when Jack emerged from the office into the sunlit August evening. He climbed in and strapped himself in with the words, addressed to the instrument panel: "A lot of people don't like flying with me because I work them too hard, but I don't really give a damn. If you want to fly with me or not, that's up to you. Now let's get this thing off the ground." His fingers buzzed among the knobs and switches. "I assume you know how to go through the checklists," he went on as we taxied out, "so let's get the wheels off the ground and get some use out of the time." I riffled my mental files until I came to the one marked "Instructors, military and style of instruction," and refreshed my memory on its contents.

As we turned out onto the runway for an instrument takeoff under the hood, he remarked: "Don't try to impress me, because it's a very long time since I've been impressed. Just do your best." I thought: "Lay off, man! All I'm asking is for you to teach me to fly. It's a very long time since I've felt the need to impress anybody and, at $60 an hour for instruction, do you suppose I'm going to do anything other than my best?" I sighed internally and applied myself to the task at hand. But that was just Jack laying down the rules so everyone knew where they stood—right now. Why waste words?

Fortunately my instrument takeoff was as straight as an arrow, and perhaps in the right seat an eyebrow rose a thousandth of an inch. We climbed straight out to the west. As we climbed through 1,800 feet, Jack said, "Level off at two thousand feet and forty-five knots." I had rarely flown at 45 knots in any circumstances, let alone on instruments. I managed it after some experimentation.

Experimentation was not good enough. What was required was the ability to set the correct power at once and by ear only. We went through the whole sequence on the instruments: turns, steep turns, climbs, descents, climbing and descending turns. From level cruise at 90 knots at 2,500 feet heading 315°, we enter a 500-feet-per-minute descent at 70 knots and level out at 2,000 feet heading 135°—all to be done smoothly and precisely. Jack was testing out the stranger who had come to him seeking enlightenment. All these maneuvers were accompanied by an interrogation on the many foibles of aircraft in general and the Cessna 152 in particular. For me this was the beginning of a new and fascinating experience in which increasingly precise flying was demanded, and failings probed and eradicated.

We landed. Jack's verdict was not long in coming. "You fly quite good instruments, young man, although you could be a lot better. If you fly with me, your instrument flying will improve very quickly."

My verdict waited until we were doing the paperwork inside the club building.

"Well?" asked Jack, "Who do you want to fly with?"

"I'm looking at him," I replied. The bargain was struck.

The first thing I discovered was that there are two opposing schools of thought on how to fly an aircraft by instruments. Quite possibly the experienced instrument pilot takes in the whole picture so fast and so continuously that he is not consciously aware of which one he uses. It is not easy to describe how they differ, yet the difference is interesting.

The "primary-secondary" method is so called because it designates some instruments as primary indicators and others as secondary indicators of pitch, bank, and power. This method is set forth in the Transport Canada *Flight Training Manual* and in the Federal Aviation Administration's *Instrument Flying Handbook*. The instruments observed give only indirect indications of the aircraft's attitude. The attitude indicator (a.k.a. artificial horizon), which displays both pitch and bank simultaneously and with no time lag, is regarded in this method as an unreliable instrument full of quirks and errors. Indeed the method dates from the days when this was true.

"Attitude instrument flying" originated with the military flying high-performance aircraft. In this concept the attitude indicator steps onto center stage. The concept states that if the aircraft is placed in a certain attitude at a certain power setting, a certain performance will result. The advantage is that the attitude indicator describes the aircraft's attitude in pitch and bank at once. This method is the more obvious of the two and the easier to learn. Moreover, in the primary-secondary system inertia of the aircraft and within the instrument system introduces a set of time lags, which is one of the main difficulties in learning to fly on instruments and one of the main reasons why untrained pilots cannot do so. If the attitude indicator and tachometer are working properly, their indications are instantaneous. Once the power and attitude are set, the time lags can be left to resolve themselves. The pilot allows this to happen and checks the results.

The disadvantage of the power-and-attitude method is that the pilot comes to rely heavily on the attitude and direction indicators, which are both driven by the same power source, one that is subject to not infrequent failures, namely, the vacuum pump. The primary-secondary system relies on a broader and more interpretive scan of the six basic instruments. Therefore, the pilot who is used to flying primary-secondary will have less difficulty in converting to partial panel should his vacuum pump fail in instrument conditions because the thought process is already implanted in his mind.

Both systems have been around for a long time. I have the Royal Air Force *Instructor's Handbook of Advanced Flying Training*, First Edition, May 1943, with the name "E. A. Morrison W/Cdr" in faded ink on the cover. The chapter on instrument flying, although it does not refer to it as such, clearly follows the power-and-attitude method. But until someone writes a good history of instrument flight, the origins of each method are lost in the mists of time.

Some wonderful and expensive instruments, such as horizontal situation indicators and flight directors, display almost all the necessary attitude and navigation information on a single screen. They are easier to use because the pilot has to scan less. He need only look at and interpret the one device. And when the device fails? Then he is back to scanning the more diffuse information given to him by the surviving instruments while looking at the failed or failing instrument, trying to discover if it has gone wrong and, if so, how, while the whole flight may be going to pieces around him. Some bad accidents have resulted.

A few lessons under the hood sufficed to bring my instrument flying and use of radio navigation aids to the point where Jack considered me ready to begin learning instrument approaches.

—22——————————————

Black Boxes and White Magic

The navigation problems of the early pilots could be solved by a combination of mapreading and dead reckoning. The first flights across the Atlantic by Alcock and Brown, and later by Lindbergh, were extraordinary feats of dead reckoning, aided, in their slow aircraft flying in unknown winds, by a certain amount of good fortune. Almost all flying was initially by reference to the surface of the earth. In the 1920s it came to be realized that safe flight in conditions of reduced visibility, or indeed in cloud, was essential if the aircraft was ever to have any real utility. Gyroscopic instruments were invented, which made that possible.

This capability produced new problems of navigation. The pilot in or above cloud was deprived of ground features by which to navigate and was left with dead reckoning. After losing sight of the ground, he maintained a certain heading for a certain length of time. Then, unless he regained sight of landmarks, he did a lot of hoping. He hoped that his airspeed, heading, and timing had been accurate. He hoped that the winds aloft had been as predicted. The means of prediction were not all that good. He hoped, therefore, that he was where he thought he was. He hoped, too, that the barometric pressure had not changed greatly and that his altimeter was still correct. Because he had no radio, he could not ask. If he was flying in continuous cloud, he hoped that there would be breaks or that the cloud base would be a reasonable height above ground with tolerable visibility underneath. That was another matter about which he could not inquire once airborne.

Then he made his descent. One of two things happened. Either he broke out of cloud and found a place to land, whether at his intended destination or somewhere else. Or he descended as low as he dared in view of the terrain heights in the area where he thought he was, saw nothing but mist and rain, and climbed back up to try again somewhere else. If any of the factors on which he based his hopes were wrong, he ran a serious risk of flying into the ground, especially if there were hills about. These problems are vividly described by Jeffrey Quill in the earlier chapters of his book *Spitfire*.*

The solution was to place radio transmitters at known positions on the ground, mark them on charts, and to install receivers and display instruments in the aircraft that would tell the pilot which "beacon" he was receiving, together with information about his position in relation to that beacon. With communication radios in the aircraft, it became possible for the operator of a radio transceiver on the ground to find the direction from which the aircraft's transmissions came, and thus to give the pilot a course to steer that would bring him to the station.

The main line of development, however, has been passive ground-based "navaids," which do not require direct communication with someone on the ground. Another line of development has resulted in devices in the aircraft which are completely self-contained and need no ground beacons at all. These systems are not used in light aircraft, so we will not go into them further. The years from 1935 onward have seen the rapid development of all these systems.

Even when the pilot could navigate through cloud until he knew that he was over his destination, there remained the problem of making a blind descent along flight paths which would keep him away from obstructions until he broke out of cloud and could see the airport. In many cases he would break out into an uncertain world of rain and mist. There had to be a procedure, a series of maneuvers, which would bring him down through the cloud and deliver him almost to the runway threshold so he could land without having to blunder about in bad visibility looking for landmarks. The larger and faster the aircraft, the more important this becomes. Darkness greatly compounds these problems.

The first radio beacons, called "radio ranges," were set up in the 1930s. During the 1940s and 1950s a variety of blind navigation systems came into service. With the transistor and microcomputer, a normally equipped light aircraft today contains more electronic navigation wizardry than did the most sophisticated military or commercial aircraft in 1950.

---

* J. Quill, *Spitfire* (London: John Murray, 1983).

The first instrument approach procedures came into use in the 1930s. As more and better ground-based blind approach devices became available over the following decades and were installed at more and more airports, so, too, the procedures for their use grew in number. A huge variety of instrument approaches has evolved in a baffling blast of acronyms—NDB, VOR, ILS, DME, PAR, RNAV, VDF, and combinations of these. Each airport of any consequence has its own specially designed instrument approach procedures, ranging from one at a small airport to more than twenty at Chicago O'Hare.

Let us have a look at some of these navaids so they will not be entirely strange when we meet them again.

The NDB is simplest in concept. The letters stand for *non-directional beacon*. It is a radio transmitter which sends out a Morse code identifier and a signal saying, electronically, "Here I am if you're interested." Commercial radio stations can also be used as NDBs, and they are marked on aviation charts. The main problem is the relative infrequency with which they identify themselves and the fact that some of them do not transmit at all times. The beacon, with its name, Morse identifier, and transmitting frequency, is marked on the charts.

The aircraft's "ear" to receive the message is the *automatic direction finder* (ADF), consisting of a receiver and a dial in the instrument panel. The dial is marked off in 360 degrees around the edge; a needle is pivoted in the center of the dial like a compass needle. The needle points to where the beacon is in relation to the aircraft's nose. Thus 0° with the needle pointing vertically upward means straight ahead, 090° with the needle horizontal and pointing to the right means that the beacon is off the right wingtip, 180° means "dead astern," and 270° means "off the left wingtip."

VOR stands for *very high frequency omni-directional radio range*. What a mouthful! The original radio ranges in the 1930s gave only a rudimentary indication of direction. Then some smart boffins in the 1940s came up with a radio range that was directional and transmitted in the VHF band, and they called it VOR. Whereas the ADF needle points to the beacon in relation to the aircraft's nose, a VOR transmitter sends out an infinite number of radial bearing lines of which only 360 are used, one for each whole degree of azimuth. It stands up and yells: "The direction from me to you is thus-many degrees. Whichever direction you may be facing, you are on my thus-many-degree radial." The pilot tunes his VOR receiver, first to the VOR he wants, and then to one of the bearing lines or "radials."

The face the VOR display presents to the pilot consists of a dial with a vertical needle. The needle is free to swing left and right of a central index mark. Surrounding the dial is a ring graduated in increments of 5°, which the pilot can turn by means of a knob. If the set is turned on and tuned to a VOR transmitter, the pilot, by turning the ring until the needle centers, can find which radial he is on. Alternatively he can turn the ring so as to tune a specified radial that he wants to follow. He can then maneuver the aircraft until the needle centers, at which point he knows that the aircraft is on that radial. Once the pilot knows which radial of which VOR he is on, he can fly the aircraft on a heading that will keep the needle centered, from which he knows that he is tracking that radial.

There is, however, an ambiguity. A pilot could be flying due east (090°) with the 090° radial tuned and the needle centered and nothing would tell him whether he was east or west of the VOR. To resolve this ambiguity, a small window in the dial shows one of the words "TO," "FROM," or "OFF." If, in the case just mentioned, the pilot had tuned the 090° radial and was flying due east with the needle centered, the window would show "TO" if he was west of the VOR and thus flying *to* the VOR, or "FROM" if he was east of the VOR and thus flying away *from* it. As he crossed over the transmitter, the word in the window would flip from "TO" to "FROM." There is nothing in the system to tell him how far he is from the transmitter. Typical navaid reception distances are on the order of 50–75 miles at altitudes below 10,000 feet.

The same concept is used in the *instrument landing system* (ILS). One element is called the *localizer*. It transmits a single radial along the centerline of the ILS-equipped runway. The second element is called the *glideslope*. It resembles a localizer lying on its side transmitting its single radial at a 3° angle up the approach path from a point 1,000 feet along the runway from the threshold. The ILS-equipped aircraft has a VOR dial with two needles, one vertical for the localizer, one horizontal for the glideslope. When both needles are centered, the aircraft is exactly on localizer and glideslope. It can come barreling in from 15 miles away and break out of cloud as little as fifteen seconds from touchdown with the runway dead ahead. One, two, or occasionally three marker beacons under the ILS course cause a receiver in the aircraft to make noises and flash lights as the aircraft passes over them, and serve as milestones.

An essential piece of equipment is a *transponder*. Imagine that you are in a dark room full of people whom you know but who refuse to identify themselves. You have a knitting needle with which you jab them. You will soon have positive identification! You are an air traffic controller at a radar screen. Your knitting needle is the radar pulse. The people are aircraft and their responses are the responses of their transponders. In its passive state the transponder enhances the aircraft's radar echo. In its active state, when the pilot presses the IDENT button, it causes a number to appear beside the aircraft's "splat" or blip on the radar screen. You contact a radar air traffic controller. He replies, "Squawk ident 4272." You set 4272 on the instrument and push the IDENT button. He replies, "Radar contact," and that is that.

DME stands for *distance measuring equipment*. It is a boon to the IFR pilot. Certain VORs and ILSs have a UHF attachment which responds to interrogation by the aircraft's DME. Suppose that on a dark night out in the open, you have a friend who agrees to shout when you flash a light. If you accurately record the time when you flash the light and the time when his shout reaches you, you can calculate how far away he is. DME does the same thing electronically.

All this equipment is used to navigate from place to place in or above cloud, out of sight of the ground, and to make a blind descent or "instrument approach" at the destination airport. Each instrument approach procedure is enshrined in an 8-inch by 5-inch sheet of paper, published by the Department of Energy, Mines, and Resources in Canada and by both government and private organizations in the U.S., called an "approach plate." It is a small map with lines and numbers on it telling the user where and how high he is supposed to be at different stages in the approach, and what courses he must steer. In spite of their infinite variety, instrument approaches tend to have a certain underlying form.

The procedure has a skeleton consisting of the *final approach fix* and the inbound track from that fix to the airport, or, if the final approach fix is on the airport, inbound to it. The "outbound track" follows the same line over the ground as the inbound track but in exactly the opposite direction—for reasons we will come to in a minute. The final approach fix may be an NDB or a VOR or some other electronic means of establishing an exact position. By following the procedure, the pilot can arrive over the final approach fix, establish himself on a particular track over the unseen ground, and make his descent along that track until he breaks out of cloud with the airfield laid out in front of him. He will have made detailed inquiries and be listening on his radios to make sure that the weather is such that he will, indeed, break out of cloud as intended. But the procedure lays down a point in the approach at which he must abandon it if he cannot see to land, and states what he should do next if that were to occur.

The approach procedure is entirely passive. No one "talks the aircraft down." The bare minimum that is needed is a radio beacon transmitting from a known position on the ground, an aircraft equipped with the necessary receivers and indicators, and an adequately trained pilot. The procedure will work even with no direct communication between the pilot and the people on the ground. The pilot flies in intricate and precise choreography about the final approach fix, breaks out of cloud, and lands.

Let us say that our intrepid aviator arrives over the final approach fix in thick cloud, having found his way through the rain, mist, sundry buffetings, sensory illusions, and other good things in store for those who fly through the clouds. He has the 8-by-5-inch sheet of paper clipped to the yoke in front of him, all his radios tuned, direction indicator set by reference to the magnetic compass, brain gain adjusted to MAX, and is in all respects ready for the approach.

On crossing the fix, he turns outbound. If he wants to go to the airport, why is he turning away from it? The final approach fix is either on the airport or close to it. Because our aviator must maintain a goodly altitude until he is absolutely sure of his position by crossing the final approach fix, he is still probably 3,000 feet above the ground. He cannot cross the fix, turn onto the final approach course, prove that he is on the inbound track, lose 2,500 feet, come busting out of cloud, and land, all in the space available.

The outbound track is defined on the approach plate and, once he knows that he is on it, the pilot can descend from the altitude at which he crossed the fix to the "procedure turn altitude," which may be 2,000 feet or so above the ground. By descending at 1,000 feet per minute and tracking outbound for one minute, he can get from 3,000 feet down to 2,000 feet before rolling into the procedure turn. What is a procedure turn? Seafaring folk call it a Williamson turn. An aircraft or a ship will not flip around in its tracks. To bring the aircraft back onto a particular track, but facing in the opposite direction, some birdman who as wise as well as intrepid invented the procedure turn.

Run your finger slowly up the centerfold of this book; turn right 45° and hold that direction for one minute; then make a slow U-turn 180° to the left. Your fingertip should now be tracking back toward the centerfold again. When you reach it, turn 45° left, and your fingertip has just done a procedure turn.

The procedure turn puts the pilot back onto the outbound track but inbound toward the final approach fix. He can now pick up the ILS if there is one. If not, there may be one or more intermediate altitudes to which he can descend successively as he crosses a succession of fixes along the inbound track. The last of these altitudes, if there is no glideslope, is called the *minimum descent altitude* below which he must on no account descend unless he can see to land. If he is on an ILS glideslope, he continues his descent to an altitude called *decision height* at which he must land or miss the approach. Minimum descent altitudes may be anything from 400 to 1,000 feet above the ground. Decision heights are commonly 200 to 300 feet above the ground, at which point the aircraft will be almost over the runway threshold.

Decision height is, as its name implies, a point of decision. A "non-precision" approach procedure (one without an electronic glideslope) specifies how long the pilot may linger at the minimum descent altitude before he must either land or miss the approach, or it indicates an electronic fix at which he must make that decision.

If the pilot misses the approach, he can try again or can fly a holding pattern on a navigation fix in the hope that the weather will improve or can fly away to the alternate destination which he selected when he planned the flight. What is much more likely is that, at some point in the approach, the aircraft will emerge from cloud and will land.

The infinite number of ifs, buts, and variations are described in the IFR manuals, but that is the general form of an instrument approach. You may say, "The last time I was in an airliner, I'm sure we didn't go through all that"—and you are probably right. If it was a flight into a large airport, a traffic controller sitting at a radar screen would have given your airliner vectors to steer, and successively lower altitudes, until the pilot picked up the ILS beams and flew down them. This method of partial ground control allows a far higher rate of traffic flow than the maneuvers needed for a full instrument approach.

What is more, your airliner may have made its approach with little or no assistance from the pilot. There are systems that couple an autopilot to the ILS beams and bring the aircraft through the changes of power and attitude which cause it to alight on the runway. Because the electronic beams are unaffected by fog or darkness, the pilot may not even see the runway until after he has landed. Fully automatic landing systems were pioneered in England to give their airlines improved reliability in the appalling weather conditions prevailing there.

ILS-coupled autopilots, although not fully automatic landing systems, are not uncommon in quite small aircraft. Even the Cessna 182, which figures in this book, has an autopilot that will lock onto a localizer. The sophistication of electronic navaids, of autocoupling those navaids to the aircraft's controls, and the ingenuity with which information is presented to the pilot are without limit. So, too, is the cost of such equipment.

Even private pilots can afford to stuff enough avionics into their small airplanes to enable them to enjoy the benefits of IFR operation. The small aircraft cannot tackle the truly foul weather or climb above it all. The pilot must ask himself, "What if the engine quits, or the prop sheds a blade, or the electrical system packs up?" and there must be an answer. But still, with due caution and cunning, the light plane pilot can fly and enjoy IFR.

There is, however, one aspect which we should not forget. In the 1930s and 1940s extended flight in instrument conditions was the realm of large multi-engined aircraft. The amount of gadgetry in the aircraft was limited by the fact that not much had been invented, and the available equipment was heavy and bulky by modern standards. The crew consisted of two pilots, sometimes with a flight engineer, navigator, and radio operator as well. In a light aircraft these tasks have all converged on the pilot, who must fly the aircraft, keep an eye on his engine instruments, work communication radios to converse with traffic controllers and pick up information broadcasts, and operate and interpret three, four, or more electronic navigation devices.

Woe betide the pilot who lets it become all too much. The weather still imposes significant restrictions on light plane IFR, especially in mountain country. The wisdom of flying single-pilot IFR at night is much questioned. Nevertheless, the aircraft's capabilities are limited mostly by those of the pilot and his need to leave himself a margin in which to deal with unforeseen emergencies.

–23

Needles in a Dark Haystack

Where does the light plane fit in among the main ground-based navigational aids and procedures used in IFR operations? What is it like learning to use them?

There are regulations concerning minimum equipment for IFR operation, but they are technical in nature. The equipment is of two kinds: the six blind flying instruments and the radio navigation equipment. The blind flying instruments are the attitude indicator, direction indicator, airspeed indicator, altimeter, vertical speed indicator, and turn coordinator. These allow the aircraft to be controlled when the pilot is deprived of outside visual references, but once he is in cloud he still has to find his way. Most light aircraft have the blind flying instruments. Where they differ is in the amount and nature of the navigation equipment.

As an example, in 1983 the Victoria Flying Club owned three Cessna 152s, a Cessna 150, and four Cessna 172s, as well as a twin-engined Piper Seneca. The 152s had the blind flying panel but insufficient navigation radios to fly IFR. Few such aircraft are IFR-equipped. Two of the four 172s were IFR-equipped, one with an ILS and one without. In 1984 the Club sold one of the 172s and bought a fully equipped Cessna 182. A fair proportion of the existing fleet of four-seater aircraft is IFR-equipped; the used fleet contains an incredible variety of equipment according to the whims of successive owners. But the naive belief that an aircraft full of gadgets makes a proficient pilot is potentially lethal.

Some of the VOR receivers in the 152s would receive localizers, and the trainee could be taught many of the basic elements of IFR, such as holding patterns, procedure turns, and the first introduction to instrument approaches without recourse to more expensive aircraft. The instructor, looking outside, had to watch for other aircraft and supply much of the navigation information, while the hooded pupil glared at the instrument panel in front of him.

Jack Kaiser was a demanding teacher and did not believe in wasting his time or the pupil's money. After a few lessons on basic instrument flying, we moved on to the elements of instrument approaches. Jack knew to perfection when a certain maneuver was done well enough to move on to the next one, not dulling the pupil's enthusiasm by excessive repetition, yet ensuring that material already taught improved through practice.

The long days of high summer were over, and many a calm September day gave way to a quiet, dark night. We flew several instrument lessons at night. The relative absence of outside references improves the simulation of instrument flight. If the trainee ignores the outside world, the simulation is quite realistic, even without the hood. Besides, he can from time to time sit up, discuss a point with the instructor, and admire the view, which makes for a pleasant trip.

We lifted off in ZLG one evening as the rim of the golden western sky faded behind the island hills. We climbed to 4,000 feet and pushed out toward the sparkling lights over Vancouver. Turning back, we homed in on the Victoria VOR for some holding patterns, followed by an instrument approach of Jack's devising, and much else besides.

The aircraft's VOR set would pick up the Victoria localizer. When a VOR set is tuned to a localizer, the needle on the dial becomes four times as sensitive as when it is tuned to a VOR. A mile back on final approach an error of two dots—there being five dots on the dial each side of the center mark—represents roughly 100 feet off the localizer centerline. This figure decreases gradually to nothing at the transmitter itself. The result is that the needle becomes progressively more skittish as the aircraft flies closer to the runway threshold. When a second beam is added for glideslope, it is no wonder that the result is called a *precision* approach. Wind will drift the aircraft off the localizer unless it is flown slightly crabwise. The pilot must find the heading on the direction indicator that will keep the needle centered. Closer to the ground, the wind changes both in strength and direction, posing a continual ticklish problem. Even the gyroscope in the direction indicator precesses, causing it to drift slightly. The pilot must remember to set the direction indicator by reference to the magnetic compass before starting the approach and a good instrument precesses very slowly, but the problem remains.

I was hunched over the instruments in the warm red glow of the cockpit lighting. The published inbound track to runway 26 was 264° magnetic, but on that heading we drifted to the right of the localizer in a light southerly wind. The needle wandered slowly toward the left side of the dial. "Try 254°," Jack suggested. The needle crept back toward the center of the dial. "Now come back to 259° and see if that will hold it." If the pilot had nothing to do but hold the inbound track, that would be plenty. The wind shifts and weakens; there is a brief jolt of turbulence; the needle becomes more and more sensitive closer to the runway; even a big truck on the highway under the final approach will cause the needle to twitch.

The pilot must also keep track of his altitude, descent rate, and elapsed time inbound from the final approach fix, because his life depends on these things. Should he concentrate on one item a split second too long, or even allow an extraneous thought to cross his mind, the others will do their best to get out of hand.

Times without number the Voice from the right seat jabbed my eardrums. Its tone left me in no doubt that a spectral hand had appeared on every television screen within 5 miles to etch the words in letters of fire and blood: "This aircraft is OFF the localizer by HALF A ¶ ß ≠ @ % DEGREE. Now get it the #@$%¢ back on and quit wandering aimlessly all over the @%$#¢ sky." Jack never liked doubt to cloud the minds of his pupils.

"Hold the aircraft still!" (We are flying through the night at 100 mph.)

"Now don't do anything crazy." (Such as letting the aircraft yaw by a single degree.)

We flew back and forth over the runway and through the 5 miles of dark sky at each end, inbound on the localizer front course, outbound on the back course, procedure turn, inbound on the back course, outbound on the front course, procedure turn, inbound on the front course again, until it was time to go home. Localizer back course approaches are the bane of instrument students.

A localizer transmits a "front course" and a "back course." Imagine someone shining a flashlight toward you and you walk toward him along the beam. You are inbound on the flashlight front course. But imagine that the flashlight also emitted a dimmer beam out of its other end; that beam is the back course. Flying inbound on the back course, the localizer needle deflection is reversed. If the needle is off center to the left, it means that the back course beam being followed is off to the aircraft's right. It follows that the pilot must not become confused as to whether he is on the front or back course, and whether in- or outbound.

The commercial pilot license in Canada requires that the candidate shall have received 25 hours of instrument dual instruction, although it does not specify what material is to be covered. Jack's instrument training went far along the road to the instrument rating. The culmination was an IFR trip in a Cessna 172, ZXP, to Vancouver and Abbotsford one calm, clear night.

We filed an IFR flight plan. The process of checking the aircraft before flight became longer and more involved. The whole stack of avionics had to be switched on, tested, and set. During the taxi the blind flying instruments had to be checked. Ground Control spoke up: "Zulu X-Ray Papa I have your clearance." We got him to wait until we stopped at the run-up point.

"Zulu X-Ray Papa ready to copy."

"ATC clears Golf Zulu X-Ray Papa to the Vancouver airport, Victor three three eight, climb to and maintain four thousand, contact Vancouver Departure on one two zero point five when clear, transponder code three seven two four." I scribbled it all down and read it back.

"Zulu X-Ray Papa your readback is correct."

We roared off toward the last light fading over the mountains and rolled into a climbing right turn toward the Victoria beacon. From there we would turn north along the airway called Victor 338, which led to the Vancouver VOR.

Never having done so much all at once, I was all fingers and thumbs, especially when trying to manipulate the microphone, a flashlight, and a pencil as well. Jack talked me through it and worked the radio. At this stage, flying the aircraft on instruments with any degree of precision was a full-time job. I wondered if I would ever do this in addition to conversing on the radio, writing down clearances, working the avionics, and keeping overall control of the flight. Jack liked to have his pupils fly the aircraft with smooth precision, work the avionics, converse with air traffic control, and also talk to him about some extraneous subject. How well the pupil did these things and how long he could keep up the juggling act before dropping a ball was a measure of his progress.

Never was there a stage in my flight training when I was not attacked by savage self-doubt, when there was no wail of disillusionment ranging from, "I'll never learn to fly" to, "I'll never be an instrument pilot." After the first few iterations I learned to ignore these voices and get on with the job of learning.

There was little traffic abroad in the calm, dark sky. The Vancouver controller picked us off the airway with vectors to the ILS.

"Where are we?" asked Jack.

"Boundary Bay," I shot back, seeing a line of blue taxiway lights below us in a glance outside. (How am I supposed to know? It's dark out there.)

I hunkered down over the instruments, forgot about such VFR landmarks and substituted vectors and navaids. The controller gave us successively lower altitudes and courses to steer to intercept the localizer. A good many things happened in quick succession, but the result was that Jack directed me to look up, and there was the main runway at Vancouver laid out before us, blazing with light. We declared a missed approach and climbed away without landing. Radar vectors pointed us toward the White Rock NDB, and we were left to our own devices.

We found our way to Abbotsford, where Jack coached me through a touch-and-go landing. Converting from instrument to visual flight close in on final approach to an unfamiliar runway at night is not exactly a skill that most people are born with. The newly licensed instrument pilot can legally take off into a low overcast at night, fly for a couple of hundred miles on instruments, and shoot an approach into an airport where there is a 300-foot overcast, a strong crosswind, and visibility of a mile in rain and fog. Lessons such as this showed me that such a flight would be by no means wise. After making another approach and bouncing off the runway once more for good measure, we headed for home.

An instrument departure at night is a strange experience. The approved method of getting airborne was to accelerate to best rate of climb speed and then raise the nose briskly by 6°. At the same time, you locked your eyes onto the instruments, and there you were—flying. You knew that the ground, unseen, was close below but that with each passing second the aircraft was lifting deeper into the sky. Out in front was nothing but dark air. All of our previous conditioning cries out against running with closed eyes, yet such is instrument flight.

It is a colossal act of faith that there really is nothing out there. I drew a macabre sense of comfort that if there was, the discovery would likely be painless. It is an act of faith, too, in the aircraft and its intricate electronic and pressure-sensing systems and in one's ability to control it. The human with his aircraft wings and the aircraft with its human brain become as one, speaking, listening, answering, sensitive antennae tuned at will to the radio beacons on the ground.

Even the IFR charts are different from those for visual flight. Ground features, if marked, are of ghostly grays and greens, that other world seen fleetingly through the rain and mist and racing cloud. The chart is of straight lines, numbers, codes, and of brief, cryptic annotations, a chart of the radio beacons.

Vancouver Terminal remarked that our transponder had packed up, which added to certain other minor malfunctions. Hostile muttering from the right seat pattered in my headphones. The Flying Club's aircraft were maintained to a high standard of perfection by a skilled and dedicated maintenance engineer named Mel Price. Mel was a silent, understated character whom you might see if you turned your head very quickly. Diplomacy was somewhere toward the back of Jack's operations manual, and relations between the two men had their ups and downs—to the secret amusement of bystanders.

"Zulu X-Ray Papa is cleared to the Victoria airport, Impor route, maintain four thousand, contact Victoria tower on one nineteen seven Impor inbound." The most intriguing feature of the mass of information on the IFR charts was the little triangles identified by bizarre names. West of Vancouver there was a clutch of them called Bajol, Briol, Canry, Jorja, and Faxto. North of Williams Lake there was a trio called Drago, Runny, and Lieky. They are none other than spectral milestones in the sky formed by the intersections of certain bearing lines from specified beacons. Our objective, Impor, was formed by the intersection of the 209° radial from the Bellingham VOR and the 154° radial from the Vancouver VOR.

We were already flying along the Bellingham 209° radial, so to pick up Impor we tuned the Vancouver VOR on the other set, turned the dial ring to receive the 154° radial, and waited for the needle to center. After resting against the right peg, it twitched furtively as we approached the radial. It sneaked out across the dial as if it hoped we would not see it. Its slow movement was easy to miss. The approach plate stated that, after crossing Impor, we could let down from 4,000 feet to 2,100 feet for the transition to the Victoria ILS. Because ZXP had no glideslope, we could use only the localizer. Turning onto the localizer, we could let down again from 2,100 feet to 1,350 feet, which had to be maintained until crossing the Victoria beacon.

The ADF needle wavers and then swings to point astern as we cross the beacon; the pace quickens. Note the time crossing the beacon because it is two minutes and twelve seconds to the missed approach point. Keep the aircraft straight. Bring back the power to 1,500 rpm and start down for 400 feet, which is the minimum descent altitude for this approach.

"Zulu X-Ray Papa the beacon inbound."

"Zulu X-Ray Papa cleared to land."

"Zulu X-Ray Papa."

Tune the Yankee NDB on the ADF and check the localizer needle. Will 264° still hold it, or is there a wind down here? Maybe 260°. And watch the second hand on the clock. And watch the altimeter.

From the right seat: "Two six zero was the heading. You're on two five eight. Get back on it."

"Come two degrees right. Hold the aircraft still."

We level off at 400 feet and chug on for a while.

"What's the time-to-see?"

"Er—one minute forty-five seconds."

"Look up."

And there is the runway just ahead.

Oh yes, it is a long, tough road, let me tell you, from being able to maintain control of the aircraft by instruments to flying an instrument approach, and a longer one yet from there to becoming a proficient IFR pilot.

"Well, young man," said Jack, as we disentangled ourselves from the headphone leads, "I like the way you handle an aircraft at night."

24

Further and Better Particulars

With our night IFR flight to Vancouver, Jack had gone as far as he intended with instrument training. He now turned the searchlight of his attention on my ability to perform maneuvers in visual flight. Searchlights have a propensity for illuminating that which is more comfortably left in darkness.

We took ZLG to the practice area. My attempt at a steep turn drew the sarcastic inquiry, "Fly Spitfires much?" followed by a demonstration of a vertically banked turn in an aircraft which theoretically would not fly in a vertical bank. There was a difference in technique, too. Doug's way of flight had been, "If you're kind and gentle to airplanes, they'll be kind and gentle to you,"—which reflected his personality. Jack did not give a damn whether the aircraft was kind and gentle to him or not. He grabbed it by the scruff of the neck and made it do exactly what he wanted.

My previous notion of slow flight had been straight-and-level flight and gentle turns at 55 knots, the aircraft's nominal stalling speed being 41 knots. The Jack Kaiser definition was a corkscrewing series of climbing and descending turns at 42 knots—exactly. The morning had been cool, but working at these maneuvers in the warming haze had me sweating buckets. My toes were a squidgy mess.

Next came stalls without number. Most people think stalls have to be learned merely to avoid them, and leave it at that. Wrong again! Each one had to be followed through until the aircraft had abjured flight with the vehemence of an alcoholic swearing off liquor. The recovery of flight had then to be carried out smoothly.

Spiral dives were no mere descending spirals. The aircraft had to stand on its ear as though sucked down a plughole in the sky, the occupants' cheeks sagging like bulldog jowls. The recovery had to consist of exactly the right control pressures in exactly the right sequence.

Doug had taught me precision spins with a gentle autorotation out of a stall straight ahead. Not so! Power off, nose up, 50 knots, stall the aircraft with full up-elevator—Bam!—full rudder—Bam!—and the aircraft reared up and capsized into a full-blooded spin. "Like that," said Jack, "otherwise a 152 won't spin properly." Once more he picked up the aircraft by its ears and threw it squalling and kicking over the edge— a kaleidoscope of tumbling green fields mixed up with bits of sky.

"OK," said he, "the engine just quit." I set up a gliding approach to a large rectangular field. "No, not *that!* Go in *there!* That's an airfield." "There" turned out to be a curved slot in the trees with none of the usual attributes of an airfield. Set up for final approach, I reached for the flap switch. "The flaps don't work." We sailed on beyond the appointed landing spot. Comment soon followed.

"Doug taught you to use judgment, didn't he? When he was teaching you, he had 17,000 hours. Right now you don't have any judgment, so you do it by the numbers, like this." "This" was a precise, set-piece maneuver, and it worked like a charm.

The next item on the menu was to make an approach to land in a field. The field selected was a long, rectangular one in a valley bordered by forested hills. Jack stated that there was an imaginary cloud ceiling at 900 feet. The field elevation was about 400 feet, and there was a 900-foot hill just off the approach end. The only feasible approach was to fly around the back of the hill, sneak through a gap on final approach, and land. We threaded our way through the gap, flaps fully extended, sliding over the blue-green crests of the cedars.

"We'll miss the one on this side," Jack remarked. "Are we going to miss the one on your side?" Now it was my turn for some fun.

"Probably," I replied nonchalantly. I was not disappointed.

"WE'D #$%¢¢$ WELL BETTER MISS IT."

We wafted in over the treetops and floated down toward the field. Just before we touched down, Jack gave the direction: "Overshoot!" At full throttle I held the nose down to pick up speed. We were charging across the field a mere 50 feet above the ground toward some low power lines. I knew that I had only to release my forward pressure on the yoke and we would bound up over them. That got Jack's attention, too. He reckoned that we had better return to the sky where we belonged. We proceeded sedately homeward.

I had a good deal to think about as I sipped hot tea from my thermos beside the airport fence and watched other people fly. No one likes to be told that his existing skills, which he has striven to attain, are inadequate. Nevertheless, I had to look facts in the face and recognize that this was so. Putting a more charitable light on it, the rules had changed. The standards had become higher. If I wanted to benefit from this man's colossal experience, I would have to absorb whatever he wished to teach, by whatever means he chose to teach it. If he said that certain standards were required, who was I to argue?

Beneath a brash and occasionally downright offensive exterior, Jack Kaiser was not only supremely skillful but also highly sensitive as an instructor. Many, if not most, instructors teach people to fly airplanes. Jack's business was making pilots out of the diverse material which presented itself to him. Few, if any, civilian organizations come close to the military in teaching practical skills. Jack had not only been a military instructor; he had trained military instructors. Each minute of each lesson was a closely controlled exercise in instruction. Jack could throw any problem at a trainee, knowing exactly how that trainee would react and what lessons were to be drawn therefrom. If the pupil turned out only to be along for a ride, a parting of the ways soon followed. The thoughtless, incompetent, the "hundred-hour-aces" burned up in the flames of his contempt. His instruction often resembled a surgeon's scalpel, probing a misconception, scraping out a bad habit, cutting out mistakes and replacing them with sound material. Even if the process hurt at times, the acquisition of knowledge was considerably less painful than the consequences of ignorance.

When work was slack, I took a week off at a time to hammer away at flight training. A stable high-pressure weather system was firmly in place. It was the season of slash fires in the woods, and the lower air became a turgid mass of smoke and haze. Climbing above all this to 5,000 feet laid open a view across a bluish white plain through which the higher mountains, dusted with the first snows of autumn, stood up like islands into the sparkling sky. My logbook was inscribed with an endless succession of "slow flight, steep turns, circuits and landings, spins, slow flight, stalls, spins, practice forced approaches, steep turns, circuits and landings." By dint of much effort, I brought my performance of these maneuvers to the general vicinity of Jack's exacting standards.

Jack's notion of flight was simple. Either you had the aircraft under control or you did not. If you were told to fly a series of corkscrews at 42 knots, that was what you did. To allow the airspeed to rise to 45 knots at some stage in the maneuver was "total-and-complete-loss-of-control-[elaborate blasphemy]-not-very-fussy-about-who-they-send-solo-these-days."

Spins were such a normal part of the agenda that I found myself stifling a mental yawn as Jack dumped us into yet another one, to demonstrate some point of airmanship, and the green fields went around and around down there in the haze. And there were stalls, out of straight flight, and climbs, and turns, and climbing turns, and descending turns, with flaps, without flaps, power on, power off. At all times the stall had to be complete and the recovery smooth. While I toiled away at these evolutions, a quickfire stream of questions came over the intercom:

"How many knots above stalling speed does the stall warning sound?"

"Why do you hold off aileron in a climbing turn?"

"Why does V_a decrease instead of increase with a decrease in gross weight?"

"How do you calculate the increase in V_a with increased g loading?"

"How many g do you pull in a level 45°-banked turn?"

"What is the stalling speed in that turn?"

"What are the positive and negative limit load factors for this aircraft?"

"Are they the same with flaps extended and, if not, why not?"

And so it went on.

We scheduled a lesson for nine o'clock in the morning on the Thanksgiving Day holiday. The previous evening I had imbibed with friends a little too heavily, not of the bottle, as might be supposed, but of the coffee bean. Consequently I slept for an hour and awoke unrefreshed. I was at the point of canceling the lesson but decided to press on, if only to see if my performance would suffer. It did.

It was a mild, damp morning with a high overcast and low-hanging patches of mist. We took UZR, a misty-blue airplane on a misty-blue morning. The turn coordinator was markedly sluggish when we tested it on the taxiway. It would only gradually return to its neutral position when we straightened out from a turn. Some of the blind flying instruments will show indications on the ground as the aircraft weaves its way out to the active runway. The pilot must, therefore, ensure that the instruments which should be indicating something are indicating in the right manner, and those which should not be indicating anything on the ground are not doing so.

We lifted off. At 400 feet on went the hood. My performance went from bad to worse. My brain had the sharpness of a lump of clay. An orientation exercise to the Victoria VOR produced bizarre results. Learning to extract the maximum utility from a VOR has its problems in any case. In my unslept condition it was downright impossible.

Jack pulled two suction discs from his pocket and covered the attitude and direction indicators. He told me to orientate to the VOR using partial panel only. The snag is that, without the gyrostabilized direction indicator, the pilot is left with only the magnetic compass and all its unstable gyrations. The only way to turn from one heading to another is, first, to figure out whether to turn left or right, next by how many degrees, next for how long, then make the turn, straighten out, let the compass settle, and read it.

If the air is rough, it will not settle. If the pilot lets the aircraft yaw while he is reading it, it will not settle either. If he is maneuvering on instruments, partial panel, the turn coordinator is the only instrument that will tell him when he has straightened out. If that instrument is sluggish, he will continue to roll out of a turn in one direction into a turn in the opposite direction without knowing it. Life can become quite difficult. The amount, nature, and volume of comment from the right seat attained alarming dimensions.

I suppressed a flash of straight anger. I knew I was putting up a rotten performance. I was furious, both with myself and with this stupid little airplane, which I knew was laughing at me. UZR was always doing things like that, but there was nothing to be done except to sit tight and make the best of a bad job.

Next came "recovery from unusual attitudes" on the instruments, an exercise replete with wingovers and spiral dives. After I had fought the airplane into submission, off came the hood and: "Your engine just quit." This is a demanding sequence in which the trainee is tumbled about on the instruments and then has to make the transition to visual flight 1,500 feet above the ground and go straight into a forced approach while he is still collecting his wits and trying to figure out which way is up, where he is, which way the wind is blowing, and good things like that.

In a glide a Cessna 152 loses 650 feet per minute, so from 1,500 feet it will be on the ground one way or another in 2 1/2 minutes. Time is not plentiful. The intention was to simulate a descent out of turbulent cloud with a failed engine and, hence, inoperative gyro instruments. The purpose was to ensure that the commercial pilot had the ability to land, cat-like, on his feet.

We glided and circled down among the patches of mist which clung to the ground. Climbing away, we punched through one just for kicks. When we returned to the ground, I admitted what Jack already knew: that it was the morning after the night before. Even so, he paid me a backhanded compliment: "Someone else would never have noticed, but I know you, and I could see you weren't up to scratch."

—25————————

Blowing in the Wind

October came and went. Autumn turned to winter. As November arrived, the weather turned wetter and more foul. "No flying: rain & low cloud" or merely "Canceled, WX" appeared more and more often in my diary. The work load at my job fluctuated, and from time to time I stole away to fly.

One Monday morning I made my way to the airport, increasingly discouraged by a strong wind. It was a cold, blustery autumn morning. Fifteen knots was the strongest wind I cared to tackle in a Cessna 152. The ATIS was reporting 18 knots gusting 22. There was little activity. Only a solitary Cessna 152 was grinding its way around the circuit, rising, falling, and dipping its wings like a leaf in the gale. I went out onto the flight line to observe its erratic progress. The wind blew wrinkles on the puddles; the aircraft were rocking at their moorings. To my mind, if an aircraft was rocking on the ground I had no business trying to fly it.

The airplane gave up its antics, landed, and taxied in to the Flying Club. Jack Kaiser and George Molnar climbed out. George and I had attended commercial pilot groundschool together. Now George was learning to be an instructor. Anyone aspiring to teach flying had to be (a) insane, (b) Batman's brother, or (c) both, so I about-turned and pushed through the wind back into the Flying Club. George and Jack came in, windblown.

"Going flying?" asked Jack breezily, as he saw me staring morosely out of the window.

"Was. Until I saw how windy it is," I replied, putting rootlets into the floor.

"Nonsense!" he burst out. "Get your ass off the ground! Go and fly crosswind landings! The weather's ideal!"

I goggled at him in disbelief. As he was beginning to emit red fumes, however, the course of prudence seemed to be to vacate the building by the nearest exit. Grabbing my gear, I promptly did so and found myself on the flight line. The wind was by now blowing ripples in the asphalt. Previously only Cessna 152s had been rocking in the wind. Now I shot a glance at our Cessna 182 and saw that it, too, was rocking and dancing at its tiedown. I clung to IMH's exterior as I preflighted it, leaving claw marks in the paint. I loosened first one tiedown rope and then the other, noticing with surprise that the aircraft did not at once do a tumbleweed act across the airfield. Having started the engine, I felt sure that my request for taxi clearance would vanish in the wind before the radio waves reached the tower, but enough of them survived to attract attention.

I took off on runway 13, straight into the gale, and tried a few circuits on that runway. Taking a deep breath, I asked for and received a clearance to essay a landing on runway 08. All went well. Little by little, I unclamped my iron, sweaty grasp on the yoke while the aircraft rolled and pitched in the turbulence. I realized that the bumps and bangs of earlier flights in strong winds were nothing more than the reaction of my tense muscles. Now I knew that the aircraft could not fall; I would not lose control. I relaxed. I sat like a sack, absorbing the turbulence, not fighting it. I had discovered that I could take off and land a Cessna 152 in a 45° crosswind of 18 knots gusting 22. After a while I landed, my self-confidence much enhanced.

"Stalls, spins, slow flight, steep turns, circuits, practice forced approaches, stalls, slow flight, steep turns, stalls, spins, practice forced approaches" read my logbook monotonously. I was making my run at the commercial flight test and had no plans to fail it.

My home in Sooke was an hour's drive from the airport, on the far side of a range of hills. The weather was often diametrically opposite in the two places, and this was important to know. Some of the girls who worked behind the dispatch desk at the Flying Club had limited aeronautical knowledge, so I developed a set of questions to ask over the telephone before leaving home.

"Is anyone flying?" (Or are the birds walking?)

"Who are they, and what are they doing?" (Are they sane persons or instructors?)

"Is the weather clear toward the practice area?" (Like the dove from the ark, has anyone departed the circuit recently and not returned?)

"Can you see the top of Saltspring Island?" (2,000 feet)

"Can you see the top of Mount Newton?" (1,000 feet)

"Are those dingle-dangles outside the window ringing?" (wind more than 10 knots)

"Are they still there?" (Or have they carried away in the storm?)

From the answers I could gain a fair picture of the weather, although the Scripture According to Murphy says that weather will deteriorate more and faster than it will improve.

The weather, hitherto quite flyable locally, if not exactly good for cross-country VFR, was now deteriorating in earnest. Needing to maintain the pressure of practice and training, I flew as often as I could. One dark afternoon I took off for the woods and scattered fields around Duncan to practice forced approaches, which were my weakest maneuver. As I prowled through the rain and gathering dusk, wind and turbulence added to the challenge. I wondered if the ground-pounders on the Trans-Canada Highway, following the shimmer of their headlights on the wet road, even noticed the little airplane gliding down silently in the rain.

Looking up the Cowichan Valley, I could see that the storm had advanced, growing blacker and wilder, and the veil of rain thicker. The rain was spreading along the mountains south of the valley, trying to outflank me. Run, little airplane, run for home in the fading light and the rising storm! I landed in a stormy dusk as the front came marching down out of the mountains.

Toward the end of November, Jack and I took off one Saturday afternoon for what was supposed to be the pre-flight-test check ride, on the basis of which he would pronounce me ready for the commercial flight test. The weather was appalling, with strong winds, a cloud ceiling at barely 1,500 feet, and heavy rain. As soon as we were decently airborne, on went the hood. Once in a while I sneaked a glance outside to see rags of cloud swirling about us. Rain rattled on the windshield like flying grit. After a short period of this, Jack uttered an oath and we turned to other things.

"Hood up. Your engine just quit. Land on that airstrip there. *What* airstrip? That there. Yes, *that*. Now don't go too close to the house because the guy's wife hates airplanes."

"Why did he marry her then?"

"Oh, she's a cute little thing, but she hates airplanes. Now stay the #$%¢*# over this side of the field or I'll strangle you."

"I'm trying to stay out the the #$%¢@ trees. What the $#¢&% do you think I'm doing? I can't see a thing."

"OK, now overshoot, and don't make too much noise or I'll never hear the end of it."

This dialogue occupied the short space of time it took to glide down in the pouring rain from 1,200 feet toward a narrow slot cut in the trees, barely a wingspan wide, which some character used as an airstrip. Through the rain-splashed windshield I could see a green-black mass of trees but no detail, and had no idea of how close to them we were. We missed them anyway.

We headed back across the Saanich Inlet at less than 1,000 feet. Of course it was an excellent opportunity for crosswind landings. Jack's verdict on this sequence came when he filled in the assessment book after the lesson.

"I'm going to give you fives for those landings. I only give fives when I could not have done better myself." Fives were not easy to come by.

The day of judgment appointed for the flight test came around. The weather was terrible. Having seen the unbelievable weather in which John Addison had administered a private pilot flight test only a few days before, I waited as the morning wore on. The cloud ceiling grew lower and blacker; the rain fell more heavily. At midday I could stand it no longer and telephoned the Flying Club to find out if John really wanted to fly the test in those conditions. It turned out that he had been waiting for me to show good judgment by canceling the test. We arranged the test for the next day. I had to work in the morning but left at noon for the airport. I was too relaxed. The final check ride had been a breeze. I had had to concentrate on my work in the morning. My brain was at "Standby," not "On."

The test closely resembled the private pilot test. The only significant addition was instrument flying under the hood. The required orientation to the Victoria VOR was done without the hood on and, because the VOR transmitter was sited in plain view on top of a prominent hill, it was not exactly a great feat of airmanship to get the aircraft pointed at it. I had practiced forced approaches on every field in the neighborhood for a week, no doubt to the alarm and annoyance of the local inhabitants. Therefore, only a certain word of four letters written in black smoke all across the sky would adequately have expressed my chagrin when my attempt at this maneuver, had it been in earnest, would have left us roosting in some apple trees.

John said remarkably little as we deplaned. I dragged my weary feet toward the Flying Club, fully prepared for the worst. One of the girls behind the desk asked brightly, "Did he pass?" To my great surprise, John nodded as he reactivated his pipe, turned to me almost as an afterthought, held out his hand, and said: "Congratulations." Everyone present showered congratulations on me, but I was so wrung out that I could utter only incoherent grunts and stare blankly into space.

Flying was not the only prerequisite for the commercial license. First, the candidate had to pass a medical examination that was marginally stiffer than the private pilot medical. As in all aviation medicals, eyesight was the great destroyer of hopes. At the private pilot stage eyesight that is less than perfect may cause a lengthy battle with bureaucracy but is seldom grounds for outright rejection. At the commercial stage the standards are higher.

Concurrent with flight training was groundschool. The course is long and hard, culminating in a written examination with the same characteristics. This particular groundschool course consisted of eighteen three-hour sessions on Tuesday and Thursday evenings between September 11 and November 6, 1984. The subjects covered were nominally the same as in the private pilot course—air regulations, engines and airframes, theory of flight, aircraft performance, navigation, flight planning, and meteorology—but they were taught in considerably greater depth. Fifteen of us started the course; about ten finished. A high degree of motivation was essential to success.

The written examination was three hours of multiple choice questions. It was a tough, slogging affair, and many people failed it. Further, it was important to complete the whole course, flying and groundschool, within a year of the date of enrollment. This went into The Files. What the penalty was for failing to do so escapes me at present, but the resulting entanglement with bureaucracy was sufficient penalty in itself.

What was it all worth? Paradoxically, the private pilot gained more from winning a commercial license than did the aspiring professional. People asked me if I wanted to fly for a living. "Of course not!" I replied. "They pay me a fat salary for crawling around underground in the mud and getting rocks on my head." There is no denying that meeting and conquering the challenge is enormously satisfying. That would, however, hardly justify the demands on time, money, and effort equal to those of the private pilot course.

It is said that the man who teaches himself has a fool for a teacher. The new private pilot is in this position. The abilities bestowed by private pilot flight training are quite meager and, if the newly graduated pilots continue to fly, which many do not, their abilities slip. They hang onto their flying skills by their fingertips. Some of them contribute to the accident statistics that highlight the 100- to 300-hour experience bracket as one of the most dangerous of a pilot's career. For the private pilot the training for a commercial license will tide him over this difficult period and will establish him as a competent visual pilot. Should he eventually go on to an instrument rating, the more rigorous training will stand him in good stead, as well as having fulfilled half of the instrument dual instruction required.

For the aspiring professionals on the course, the future was far from rosy. A commercial license was of little value without further ratings and endorsements such as floatplane, multi-engine, instrument, or instructor. Even with these, flying jobs were almost nonexistent and, if found, carried the most abysmal pay and working conditions. The stock response from any air carrier was: "Come back when you have a thousand hours." How the applicant was to move ahead from the 250 hours with which he finished his formal training to 1,000 hours if no one would hire him was conjectural.

Some pilots laid out $4,000 on an instructor's rating so as to build up the all-important flying hours teaching other people to fly. From what I could see, teaching flying for a living merely postponed the instructor's eventual death by starvation. I made the cynical suggestion to one young hopeful: "Why don't you go and drive a garbage truck? Then you can afford all the flying you want." The supply of pilots always exceeded demand, and times were tough in western Canada in 1984.

—26————————————

A Spreading of Wings

There comes a time—there must come a time—when the fledgling pilot lays out a map on a table, or charts on the floor, and lets his eye roam over the land thus depicted. Curious, he juggles some numbers—speed, time, fuel—and then he spreads his wings and flies. He flies far beyond the landmarks of home. He flies not with an instructor or even a friend. He flies not where his instructor told him to fly. He pushes out into his unknown.

I was slow to do this. For me an aircraft was a creature which took me into the sky. Any piece of sky would do. The land or water surfaces beneath, and the works of man, were sometimes interesting, amusing, something for casual observation, but ultimately they were the bottom of the sky and nothing more. If humanity called one group of things on the ground "Seattle" and another "Vancouver," what of it? In places the land stuck up and occupied large volumes of otherwise perfectly usable airspace, and that was a problem. But I did not bemoan the fact that the mountains occupied so much sky, because life without them was not worth living and there was plenty of sky around and between them, enough for everyone. But there was this thing about sky.

I loved the dark sky, and cloudscapes seen from within. When the sky was clear, I loved to tumble about in it or, if nothing else offered, to pursue that elusive goal of the perfect turn, the perfect circuit, the perfect landing. And I loved the utter solitude, the utter self-reliance of flight. I had not spent nearly fifteen years as a mining engineer, mostly in underground mining, without knowing that in the depths of the mine there were things, many of them apparently innocent things, which would kill you quickly and without compassion. In the final analysis you betted your life on your vigilance, wisdom, and cunning, and when faced by dangers that no art of man could avert, you discovered that God held you in the hollow of His hand. In accepting these things, you were totally alive. In being thus alive, there was an indestructible joy. The rock and the sky, the one so hard and forever unchanging, the other so soft and forever changing; yet in the sky, too, there was this same lethality, this same lack of compassion, this same urgent demand for skill and cunning. The more I understood the challenge, the more deeply I accepted it.

But any piece of sky would do. The fact that an aircraft could transport me rapidly to places where I had no reason to go had an underlying absurdity. Indeed later, as an instrument pilot, I would file an IFR flight plan that expressed my earnest desire to travel expeditiously from one place to another, when I wanted nothing more than to wander among the clouds.

Certainly I enjoyed flying with other people to where their needs and fancies took them, but I could see no challenge in taking off, flying straight and level in clear skies for a certain length of time, and then landing at some airport where I had no purpose in being. VFR cross-country flying was full of hazards, uncertainties, and frustrations for much of the year. In some winter months the days when it was possible to penetrate the coastal mountains under VFR could be counted on the fingers of one hand. The mountains were continually shrouded in rain and low-hanging cloud. To the south, however, lay America. On our mental aviation charts it was a blank, inscribed: "Here be dragons: caution possible wake turbulence."

The candidate for the commercial pilot license had to have completed a certain number of hours of cross-country flight, both by day and by night. To fulfill this requirement, I decided to go and visit the dragons, with due regard for their wake turbulence.

The first dragon was the U.S. Customs Service, which had to be placated because it could not be avoided. The second was the notion that ceaseless contact with air traffic controllers was mandatory at all times, which was untrue. The third was the simple fact of being in foreign airspace, which was not a dragon at all. On closer acquaintance these three dragons evaporated like the morning fog, which, in winter, hung copiously on the Pacific coast.

This February morning the weatherman said: "There's the trailing edge of a weak warm front moving down Puget Sound, giving thousand-foot ceilings and restricted visibility in rain. . . . Tomorrow? . . . . Let's see now. . . . There should be some ridging and, yes, conditions in the Seattle area will definitely be better." The trip had to be delayed until the next day, but such is VFR. The next morning broke with masses of fog hanging on the cool air still saturated from the day before. The warmth of the spring sun pried them apart until by the middle of the day only the most obdurate remained.

There were airfields called Airports of Entry, which were continuously manned by Customs officials. There were Landing Rights Airports, where Customs clearance could be arranged, sometimes with great difficulty or not at all. There were airports with no Customs facilities at all. Any Customs clearance had to be arranged well in advance by telephone at long-distance rates. Several directories of U.S. Customs telephone numbers were available for aviators, but a succession of aggrieved and uncomprehending voices proved that every published telephone number, without exception, was wrong.

Customs officials at Landing Rights Airports were available on weekdays only, and then not always. They enjoyed their midday siesta like the rest of us. At this season of the year, the time between the disappearance of the morning fog and the beginning of the U.S. Customs lunchbreak was not very long. The only accessible Airports of Entry were in the Seattle area, and to enter Seattle airspace required a transponder. Most Flying Club aircraft did not have transponders. No problem of air navigation will ever baffle or frustrate the pilot as much as his efforts to navigate through the thickets of ground-bound bureaucracy, which sprouts on the aviation business like fungus, and to similar effect. Nevertheless, once a workable procedure could be found, the inhabitants of this particular thicket were friendly.

The next question was the infinity of radio waves that criss-crossed the atmosphere at all manner of different frequencies. The back flap of the Seattle chart listed sixty. In the mostly empty skies of Canada, unless you were in contact with someone at an airport directing traffic, you listened on 126.7 MHz and that was that. It was amusing to hear American pilots asking "Victoria Approach" who to contact next as they were cast loose into the Great Canadian Wilderness because there was no one to be contacted. I was obsessed with the reverse problem. Who am I supposed to be talking to? How do I know which of these sixty frequencies to use? What are the consequences of talking to the wrong person? What are the consequences of not talking to anyone?

The procedure turned out to be easier than I had feared. Outside the control zones surrounding airports it was not necessary to talk to anyone. Although radar air traffic controllers had my echo on their radar screens, they did not wish to converse with a transponderless aircraft. It was nothing but a random speck, an impurity floating in the black fishbowls of their radar screens, a hazard for their clientele to avoid. Approaching an airfield where I wanted to land, I had only to pick the control tower frequency off the chart and announce myself in the usual way. The same disembodied voices uttered the same functional welcome in the same language as they did in Canada.

American air supported the aircraft just as effectively as the Canadian variety. The sky took no more notice of man's petty differences than did the brown mountains which rose level with my wingtip.

In the early afternoon I cleared U.S. Customs at Bellingham, flew south through the quiet sky to Everett, and then across to Port Angeles. The island shadows lengthened on the silver sea. Sheets of stratus held at bay by the warmth of the sun crept from their lairs, flowing on the evening air. As other diurnal creatures turned to their homes, so did I. It had been fun meeting the folks across the fence, and never a dragon had I seen.

The Flying Club reminded me that I had to build up some night flying time before my commercial license could be issued. I had often heard of the Red Baron restaurant amongst the airport buildings at Abbotsford and set off one February evening to see what it offered. The sky was clear and quiet with the promise of a moonlit night. It was a simple flight from all points of view, and soon I was parked outside the Red Baron.

The restaurant was well appointed and the food excellent. A carafe of wine and a glass of brandy to follow would have been most welcome, but the beauty of the night sky would have to make up for my enforced abstinence. I had not the least doubt that a Frenchman would have enjoyed his wine and flown with *panache*. An Englishman would have wiped the beer froth from his moustache and flown with aplomb. A German would have drained his *Stein* and flown with *Zweckmäszigkeit*. But I had been told that instant destruction awaited those who flew with so much as a trace of alcohol in their blood, and I was not about to test the assertion. The path of the pilot is hard indeed.

By the time I went out onto the asphalt, the moon had risen. Preflighting the aircraft, I noticed that the wings were covered with frost. Trying to take off with even a sheen of frost on the wings has caused some serious accidents. The standard remedy is either anti-freeze or a heated hangar. Late on a Saturday night at Abbotsford, there was not the least chance of finding either. The next best thing would be alcohol, but I was not going to buy Courvoisier just to de-ice aircraft wings.

My gray matter warmed to the task and realized that aircraft fuel out of the sump drains would do just as well. I found a paper towel in the seat pocket, drew fuel into the sampling cup, and went to work. Each patch began to frost over as quickly as I cleaned it. The whole top surface of the wing was frosted. Now think. Why is frost dangerous? Because it causes the boundary layer on top of the wing to become prematurely turbulent, altering the flying and stalling characteristics of the wing. But at some point along the wing's upper surface the boundary layer becomes turbulent anyway. I guessed that such a point would be about as far back as I could reach while standing on the ground, about one-third chord. Using the wooden dipstick in addition to the paper towel, I scraped and scrubbed and polished.

In fifteen minutes the job was done. I scrambled into the aircraft to get air moving over the wings as quickly as possible. There was 5,000 feet of runway in which to find out if IMH wanted to fly or not. The ground roll was supposed to be 750 feet; lightly loaded on a cold night even IMH should match that. It did, although I kept a healthy margin of airspeed as I climbed away into the night.

The lower Fraser Valley was thinly covered by snow. Fields stood out as clearly as in daylight. A line of faint lights on the western horizon marked the shore of Vancouver Island. The VOR needle and compass showed me where to aim. No one else was about.

"What would you do if the engine quit?"

"Glide down into one of those fields."

"What if you were over the straits?"

"Glide straight in to the Orcas Island strip, activating the runway lights by clicking the mike seven times on 122.7 MHz."

"How do you know that?"

"Because I took the trouble to look it up beforehand. So there."

"What would you do if all the electrics quit?"

"Continue to Victoria, check for traffic, fly past the tower flashing my identification letters in Morse with the flashlight presently slung round my neck."

"Is that a standard procedure?"

"Got any better suggestions?"

"What is the code for IMH?"

".. _ _ ...."

"What if the tower didn't see you?"

"Check for traffic and land."

Having set these inquisitorial little gremlins to rest, I turned out the red cabin light and sat back to enjoy the perfect peace of the flight. The sky was utterly calm. I had only to rest a fingertip on the yoke and my toes on the rudder pedals. I could see the VOR needle dimly in the moonlight. My ears savored the smooth drone of the engine. Just you look after the engine, and it will look after you.

The islands passed beneath as darker humps on the dark sea. There in a channel were the white lights of a ship. Small orange lights nestling on the islands were the dwellings of man. Did anyone hear me droning by, far up under the moon? Perhaps another pilot looked out of his door or window to search for my navigation lights among the stars.

All too soon we came to Moresby Island, where we had to begin our descent. "Twenty-five thousand thin scattered" went the ATIS. There was, indeed, a patch of cirrus lit by the moon, a bundle of luminous fibers suspended in a sky suffused with moonglow. Of course you do not have to be a pilot to look up and see these things. It is just that, for the most part, only pilots do. We swept down in an S-curve, touched lightly on the dark runway, and taxied in to the Club ramp.

I sat for a time pondering the flight, listening to the gyroscopes running down and the engine ticking. Well might I ponder, because that was my last flight in IMH. A few months later someone landed it hard on a rough strip, damaging the nose so badly that the aircraft had to be written off, although now it stands on a pedestal beside the highway inviting people to learn to fly. I mourned that airplane. Derek had shown me a spin in it. Doug had taught me so much as we flew it together. I had passed my private pilot flight test in it. Now we had voyaged the starry skies high up under the moon.

—27—

Precision

"You think you've seen precision. You ain't seen nuthin'." These words, expressed in a forbidding snarl, were Jack Kaiser's introduction to training for the instrument rating. With my commercial license achieved and the winter skies thick with cloud and rain, it was natural to press on toward the instrument rating. The one thing I failed to take into account was the fact that 150 hours of pilot-in-command time had to be built up before the rating could be issued. At the end of 1984, I had the modest total of 107. I pressed on regardless.

The onward journey from the private license to the instrument rating is longer and harder than that from the discovery ride to the private license. It is a continuing expansion of the mind. The groundling on his first flying lesson grasps the yoke firmly in both hands, concentrating with iron will on preventing the aircraft from falling into the abyss beneath its outspread wings. He learns to use one hand for the yoke and the other for an increasing variety of other tasks. Even so, the concentration on flying the aircraft is so intense that he may be oblivious to radio messages, or even to his instructor's voice.

Gradually his mind expands so that he can fly the aircraft, talk with his instructor, and converse on the radio at the same time. No one need laugh. The novice pilot is presented with an avalanche of new sensations and mental puzzles never encountered on the ground. Moreover, he cannot rehearse them one by one. They come at him all at once.

Before learning to fly, I wondered how a private pilot on a VFR cross-country flight could possibly do all that is required of him. In due course I discovered that his awareness expands beyond the immediate business of flying to the overall management of the flight. Now I know that it is not even very difficult, provided that adequate preparations are made beforehand.

IFR operation, as distinct from instrument flying, has many stages, each of which is a further expansion of the mind. First, the pupil must learn to keep the aircraft under control by instrument references only. Then he must learn to fly to more exact standards than any required for visual flight. Next he must learn to fly precise tracks in relation to navigation beacons. This requirement does not exist in visual flight. It takes close and unremitting attention to the instruments to a degree that is not even desirable in visual flight. He must learn to read and, to some extent, memorize the instrument approach procedures. Last, he must learn to operate the formidable bank of radios that are essential to IFR operations, and to speak the IFR language.

There was IFR groundschool as well. It had been found that a Friday evening and two very full days of groundschool over the next two days were more effective than the normal series of evening classes spread over several months. I remembered private pilot groundschool eighteen months before and how few of the participants had won their wings. Even fewer of them were still in evidence as active pilots. A dozen highly motivated students had attended commercial pilot groundschool. Now there were five of us at IFR groundschool. The motivation was fierce, as was the pace of instruction. Jack Kaiser and Norm Dressler, the meteorology instructor, threw it all at us—the whole functioning of the North American IFR system. The tone of the course was precision, numbers without end, and that for all things there is a procedure. The backdrop to the course was the IFR written examination, similar in quality to the much feared and often failed commercial written exam.

My first IFR lesson with Jack since our journey through the night sky four months before bore the epitaph: "Canceled—fog." The following day he was due to take a student pilot on a navigation exercise. We fully expected the weather to be too bad and arranged an IFR trip in that expectation. The next day the sun shone from a cloudless sky.

Jack's program was to "fly" an exercise in the simulator, followed by the same exercise in the aircraft. An evening session in "the box" allowed him to remove the rust from my instrument flying with the action of a pneumatic chipping hammer.

"The box" was a generic cockpit with a lid. Beside it was a table surfaced with a simplified map of southern Vancouver Island and the lower mainland, which in turn was covered with clear plastic. A fiber-tip pen on a small trolley traced unerringly the meanderings of the pupil in the box, to his alarm and despondency when released therefrom. The most carefully "flown" tracks would resemble those of a drunken snail. Each lapse of attention, each distraction, would be mercilessly recorded.

Fortunately, the Infernal Device recorded only ground track and not the large and frequent excursions from assigned altitudes. The instructor's console allowed various instruments to fail and winds to blow the "aircraft" off course. By connections inside the works, the instructor could set up any of the two dozen navigational beacons in the area so that the dials in the cockpit would respond appropriately when the knobs were set correctly. In that way any combination of flights around Victoria, Abbotsford, Nanaimo, Vancouver, and Bellingham could be simulated.

After some flights in the simulator and various aircraft, and an introduction to ILS approaches, Jack pointed out that nothing could be gained by going any further until I had built up the required 150 hours of pilot-in-command time. I had only 120. In time, money, and effort thirty hours is a lot of flying. At the same time I had the misguided notion that "pilot-in-command" meant precisely that. The snake in the grass was that the 150 hours had to include fifty hours of cross-country flying, which necessarily had to be carried out under VFR. In the cloudy skies of spring, cross-country VFR was next to impossible with any degree of safety or likelihood of success.

But come with me into the dark sky and shoot an instrument approach. It is you in the hot seat. You are the phantom prestidigitator cruising the night sky with a fabulous four-dimensional juggling act.

"Zulu X-Ray Papa, you're cleared to the Abbotsford airport, straight-in ILS zero six approach, maintain three thousand, direct White Rock, report White Rock inbound to the tower on one nineteen four." You read it back to the controller.

"Zulu X-Ray Papa, your clearance checks."

The night is calm, dark, and cloudless. Orange and white lights on the ground spread carpet-like to the margins of the Fraser River floodplain and lap against the thicker darkness of the hills. Inside the aircraft is the red glow of the cabin lighting. The light is from the ceiling behind your head; it casts shadows in unwanted places. The engine drums through the soft hiss of static in your headphones. Your ears sweat and the headphones slip. In front of you is the wall of the instrument panel pierced by portholes in which the white needles and symbols dance and waver, twirl and skip. Your mind must take in all of them, orchestrating them with hand and foot pressures on the controls, now holding them firmly in line, now leading them into a different dance, now catching a wayward sneak trying out its own step. You have seen them all ever since you started to fly but without noticing them other than as independent entities. But then you were a yokel peeping in through the stage door. Now you are the conductor. Your instructor sits beside you, sensed rather than seen, now prompting, now reassuring, now chiding, now encouraging.

Held in a clip on the yoke in front of you is an 8-inch by 5-inch sheet of paper printed in mauve, covered with numbers and strange, intricate designs. It is headed "ILS RWY 06 ABBOTSFORD." Your aircraft is not equipped with a glideslope receiver, and you see that a procedure exists for just that contingency.

You have tuned your #1 VOR set to the Abbotsford localizer on 109.7 MHz, your #2 set to the Bellingham VOR with the ring set to the 040° radial, which cuts across the airport. You have the ADF tuned to the White Rock beacon on 332 kHz; the needle points straight ahead. "Tuning" is nothing special. The avionics are crystal-tuned, and it is a matter of twiddling the right knobs until the right numbers appear in the right windows. But there are a lot of knobs and numbers.

You are level at 3,000 feet, steering 095°. After about five minutes you see the localizer needle, which has been against the righthand stop on the dial, creep in toward the center. You would never notice its furtive motion unless you were watching for it. Just before it centers, you turn onto the inbound heading of 064°. The ADF needle, after wavering uncertainly, swings to point astern.

Your right hand eases back the throttle to 1,500 rpm, mixture full rich, carb heat hot, and you start down for 1,400 feet according to the rubric on the plate, which states: "*Straight in localizer, only, approach authorized from White Rock NDB 1400 to Abbotsford NDB." You tune 119.4 on your communication radio and transmit:

"Abbotsford Tower, Zulu X-Ray Papa White Rock inbound."

"Zulu X-Ray Papa report the outer marker," the tower controller replies.

You tune the ADF to 344 kHz for the Abbotsford beacon. Turning up the volume control, you hear: "dah-dit-dit-dah, dah-dit-dit-dah," in a low musical note which is the identifier. The needle points dead ahead to the Abbotsford NDB, which by now is about nine miles away.

While this is going on, you are descending gently through the night sky. It takes only two minutes or so to descend to 1,400 feet, and you had better remember to level off at 1,400 feet exactly or the gentleman in the right seat will have plenty to say about it—mostly far from polite at that. Just before you reach 1,400 feet, you bring the power up to 2,100 rpm and level off.

About five minutes later, after chugging industriously along the localizer at 1,400 feet, you see the ADF needle starting to move away from the 0° mark. You wonder if you should go after it. No, the beacon must be close, and, besides, it is not exactly under the localizer course. It swings astern.

You note the time on the clock, start down for 700 feet, which is the minimum descent altitude given on the plate, and transmit:

"Zulu X-Ray Papa the outer marker inbound."

"Zulu X-Ray Papa cleared touch-and-go," the tower controller replies. Here, now, you have to get on down to 700 feet and then level off.

"What's the MDA?" hisses the voice in your headphones.

"Seven hundred feet," you reply.

"Then why are we flying at seven hundred and twenty feet, twit?"

Silence.

"Just hold it steady.... Come two degrees left....Don't do anything crazy. . . . How long since we crossed the beacon?"

Of course you cannot remember where the second hand on the clock was when you crossed the beacon. The clock just stares back at you.

"Haven't a clue," you reply.

"What's the time-to-see?"

"Two minutes fifteen seconds."

"Well it's about two minutes now. Look up."

The jeweled runway is just ahead. You extend flap progressively and jockey the power. You settle into the dark chasm of the runway, now wringing lift from the wings, now adding a hint of power. Your fingertip on the throttle pushrod feels the propeller flailing the lightless air. You touch with a soft thump and a muffled chirp from the tires.

Flaps up, carb heat cold, flashglance to see that the flaps are retracting, full throttle, and you are off again into the night. Your eyes lock onto the instruments. You tune the Sumas NDB on the ADF. The beacon is just off the end of the runway, and you are over it almost as soon as you have tuned it. You roll into a climbing right turn and tune the Abbotsford beacon again as you climb higher into the dark sky.

During one such evolution Jack unburdened himself of a brief homily: "Young man, you have just flown an almost perfect approach. Not perfect, but almost. The inbound track is zero six four. To track on zero six three or zero six five would be good, but only zero six four is perfect. You will fly perfect approaches or I will personally kill you. Do you understand?" The side tone of my voice on the intercom sounded sepulchral in my ears: "Yes Jack. I understand."

Did someone say that learning to fly was easy?

Yet, to be one of Jack Kaiser's pupils and, ultimately, a "Kaiser graduate" carried a certain *cachet* for that very reason. There was the time, among many, when I was at the Flying Club, leaning on the dispatch counter, chatting up the girl behind the desk—an activity pursued by various Club members with a degree of persistence matched only by its perennial lack of effect—and chewing the rag with anyone who happened to be around.

In the room was one of our aspiring airline pilots. This kid came to flying lessons in a white shirt, black tie and slacks, and shoes you could see your face in. He was the kind who knew from the cradle that no pilot, while operating under IFR, shall operate a transponder responding to Mode A/3 interrogation other than as directed by ATC. Carried a complete set of IFR approach plates for Western Canada on pre-solo training flights out to the practice area. You know the sort.

Struck by a felicitous thought, I turned to him and remarked in a tone of voice pregnant with arcane wisdom: "Y'know, you can always spot people who fly with Jack Kaiser."

"*How?*" The word fluttered over to a point directly beneath my lips and held out small pink hands for the pearl of aviation knowledge which was obviously about to fall from them.

"By the teeth marks up and down their right arms," said I and walked away.

-28

VFR, a Very Frustrating Restriction

The VFR pilot's worst enemy is the weather. For purely local flying it may not be much of a problem, and my diary shows only a small percentage of local flights canceled for that reason. As soon as the pilot seeks to spread his wings and to travel, however, it becomes a serious and persistent obstacle. Forty percent of the fatal accidents involving single-engined landplanes in Canada are weather-related, with darkness or mountains, or both, often contributing. Further, forty percent of the fatal accidents involve private pilots who have fewer than 300 hours of flying time. Similar statistics apply to the United States. Not all are weather-related, but there is a strong implication that the weather is something the new private pilot must take seriously.

So what actually is the problem? It is twofold: turbulence and visibility. As far as the light-plane pilot is concerned, serious turbulence results from high winds or thunderstorms. Severe turbulence can throw the aircraft about so much that the pilot loses control. Less severe turbulence can cause him to bend the aircraft on takeoff or landing. More insidious is the loss of visibility.

The wise and happy pilot will put half a mile to a mile of air between himself and the hard, knobbly ground as he cruises between the legendary points A and B. Seen from that height, the land is laid out like the chart on his lap. His gaze can take in enough of the world so he need never be unsure of his whereabouts. His apparent speed over the ground is slow enough for him to carry out the numerous tasks needed for the safe and pleasant conduct of the flight. He can receive radio transmissions from distant stations, whether voice or navigation signals. Someone may have his echo on radar. If an emergency were to occur, his request for help or advice could be heard afar. His access to information by radio might well prevent the emergency from occurring in the first place. If his engine were to malfunction, he would have time either to rectify the problem or to glide to any of a selection of forced landing grounds, or even an airfield.

Under VFR in Canada, the pilot must remain within sight of the ground. American regulations allow VFR on top of cloud decks, but if the whole sky is a mass of cloud or merging layers, that is not a good or practical place to be. As the clouds become lower and more densely packed, the pilot must fly lower and the advantages of height disappear. Even if he can fly above scattered clouds, his view of landmarks, other than those directly below, is cut off and many a pilot has found the clouds closing in beneath him. Dodging clouds is the easiest way imaginable to get nowhere and get lost in the process. It also plays havoc with the time control which is essential to a carefree flight.

If the pilot decides to press on under lowering clouds, other and worse problems may arise, especially if he flies into rain, mist, or snow. With good visibility beneath a well-defined ceiling, all may be well. But flying low in poor visibility, he is presented with a kaleidoscope of landmarks, a few at a time, seen briefly and in sharp perspective. The pilot may become lost, thus increasing his risk of hitting things or of wandering about until he runs out of fuel. He may be too low to receive radio signals or to appear on a radar screen or to let anyone know of his plight. The lower he flies, trying to keep the ground in sight, the worse these hazards become. The poorer the visibility, the harder it is to see it getting worse ahead. If the pilot then flies into cloud, snow, or blinding rain, he will be lucky to escape with his life.

At night these problems are immeasurably compounded. VFR flight continued into foul weather has one common ending. The wise VFR pilot knows these things and therefore scans the weather reports carefully before enplaning on a cross-country flight, assuming that he can both understand what they say and interpret what they mean (two different things). Moreover, the cunning pilot leaves himself a margin, simply to avoid problems enroute. Interpreting the weather reports for the purposes of VFR flight is not always easy. Many sky conditions are legally VFR but are still well worth avoiding, especially over open water or mountains, or at night. A high percentage of VFR flights is canceled before takeoff or diverted enroute.

At Victoria we had the options of obtaining a weather briefing by telephone or of visiting the airport weather office in person. Some of the briefers were helpful; some were not. Before his first solo cross-country flight Harvey Taggart put his head around the door to be greeted with the question, "What the hell do *you* want?" On another occasion the briefer read the weather reports to me in quickfire style and then rounded off his dissertation, as I stammered and stuttered and tried to scribble it all down, with that most cutting of all put-downs: "Will there be an instructor aboard?" I did not even have to duck as I walked out through the crack under the door. It was not surprising that we preferred to telephone the 800 number of the Flight Service Station in Vancouver.

The qualifications for the instrument rating require fifty hours of cross-country pilot-in-command time, which must perforce be completed under VFR. My diary shows that, at the risk of being accused of excessive caution, it took me two years to complete this requirement. But there were never any hair-raising encounters with foul weather, and minimal amounts of money wasted on the 180° turn.

The fifty hours of cross-country flying involved planning thirty-seven flights. Of these, nineteen (51%) were completed as planned. The rest were canceled or diverted because of weather. There were two categories: flights planned in advance for a preset route and date, and flights planned on the spur of the moment to take advantage of fair weather. The preplanned flights show a success rate of 45%, the spur-of-the-moment flights 75%. The message is that if you pick a nice day, you will have a 75% chance of flying somewhere, provided that you do not mind where. The chances of going to a particular place on a particular day under VFR come out at less than evens. IFR capability would have increased this figure to 80%. The balance involved small airports without instrument approaches, forecast high winds, turbulence, hail, and thunderstorms. Moreover, thirty of the thirty-seven flights were planned in the summer months, the odds against successful cross-country VFR in winter being such that the effort of planning the flight was barely worthwhile. Such, statistically, is the freedom of the skies for the VFR pilot.

To moderate this harsh statement, it should be added that the utility of the light aircraft in VFR is entirely route-specific, especially in mountainous country. A dry climate, flat terrain, short routes, seasonal operations, routes flown repeatedly, and growing pilot skill all contribute to a higher success rate. But, as an example, the new pilot who learns to fly for the express purpose of flying across mountains at will all year around is, quite simply, backing a loser. The only way in which he can do that is IFR in a powerful aircraft such as a twin turboprop equipped for beating off ice. Indeed, one airline pilot friend of mine who flies twelve-seater twin-engined aircraft for a living told me he would cancel a flight if moderate or severe icing was forecast for the route. Most people forget that airline transportation achieved its present standards of safe, all-weather operation only with the advent of the turbine-powered aircraft.

I attended private pilot groundschool with a successful businessman who bought himself a brand-new Mooney with all the fixings for $110,000. The questions he asked in groundschool were terrifying in the sheer lack of common sense which they revealed. Quite soon he and the Mooney had gone their separate ways and were seen no more in those parts.

Another pupil at that same groundschool owned a business across the water. He bought himself a raggedy little Cessna 152 and used it all the time. His route was at low altitude from island to island; he knew it well; he developed lots of savvy about when not to go; and the aircraft was a thoroughly useful asset. Then there were the floatplane pilots sneaking along, a few hundred feet off the water, navigating by counting the log booms, and they achieved a high success rate. But in absolute terms the utility of the light aircraft, when flown by a private pilot restricted to VFR, is limited.

One Saturday in April, Kay Taggart had gone to a Sweet Adelines bash in Vancouver, leaving Harvey with his daughter, Beth, and the dog, Muggs, for company. Harvey and I thought we would take a Cessna 172 down to Boeing Field in Seattle, have lunch, and return via Port Angeles. I planned the flight to the mile, knot, degree, and pound of fuel. The evening sky on that Friday promised a fine day for the flight, which the weather office confirmed in the morning.

We reached the airport, however, under a gray, overcast sky. We spent some time in the Flying Club making various and sundry preparations. Harvey went across the road to buy an extra chart. When he returned with it, he remarked that it was raining. I tore outside and scanned the sky in all quadrants. It was indeed raining, and hard. A telephone call to the weather office produced the usual: "You should be OK."

"What's the big picture?" I inquired suspiciously.

"We have a frontal system over the north end of Vancouver Island due to reach Seattle around four o'clock tomorrow morning."

I went outside and stood in the rain. The effects of the front were obviously with us now, regardless of where it was supposed to be.

"Harvey," I said, "I hate to tell you this, but we're not going to

Boeing Field because very likely we won't be able to get back. The weather's turning sour at this very moment."

With an equanimity born of experience, we discussed where we should go, if anywhere. We decided to go to Abbotsford, where we could at least have lunch at the Red Baron. By now even George Molnar, who had just canceled a mountain-flying expedition because of reported 60-knot winds and mountain waves, was not too sure and telephoned for the latest Abbotsford weather. It was mediocre VFR.

We slopped around the outside of JTL in a steady rain. Taking off to the east, a gentle turn put us on course. Small puffs of cloud nestled in the hollows of Pender Island. I had planned to climb to 5,500 feet but was stopped at 5,000 by a veil of cloud.

The far shore came into sight before we left the islands. With no shore in sight, it would be easy to try it for a few more minutes while the gray-white sea merged with the gray-white stratus, fog, and rain. Stratus layers without sharp edges are invisible against other stratus or calm water. Down there, is that water or cloud? Now where is the horizon? We could easily slide into instrument conditions. I had no doubt of my ability to turn around on instruments but had no intention of getting into the situation to begin with. "Continued VFR into IFR conditions" is a common cause of fatal accidents. Looking up at puffy cumulus clouds against a blue sky, you may wonder how anyone could fly into cloud without knowing it. Looking out of an aircraft on a misty day, things are not quite so clear-cut.

Approaching the mainland shore, we could see that the lower Fraser Valley was covered by a low-hanging layer of broken cloud. The radio chatter on the Abbotsford tower frequency was obviously among VFR traffic, so we let down between the clouds. Visibility underneath was definitely on the dull side. Flying at 1,000 feet, we tracked a VOR radial which would bring us to the field. The runways eventually appeared out of the murk. The Red Baron was shut, so we had to be content with the local greasy spoon.

Meanwhile, the weather continued to worsen. The people in the Flight Service Station had long faces. A Luscombe had taken off but had soon returned. Knowing that the lowest clouds ended at the shoreline, we reckoned it was worth a try. The Victoria weather was reported as more or less flyable.

Harvey was at the controls as we lifted off into the rain. We crept along at 700 feet, just below the cloud base, keeping a sharp lookout for other aircraft whose radio chatter we could hear as they poked about in the dim light. Approaching the shore, we climbed through an avenue between the clouds in the hopes of gaining a better view. The sole result was that the horizon ahead disappeared. When the clouds began to close in beneath us as well, we turned around and ducked back down before resuming our course toward Victoria.

"Harvey?"

"Yes."

"See that oil refinery ahead?"

"Yes."

"Do you think we could avoid hitting it?"

"Probably."

Looking out across the straits, we could see only a uniform mass the color of a dirty sheet. We turned north along the shoreline with the intention of going into Boundary Bay. We felt surer of finding the airport at Boundary Bay than of returning through the murk to Abbotsford. As we flew slowly up the shoreline, listening on the Boundary Bay tower frequency, it became clear that the airport was fogged in. At the same time, we had a clear view of three islands—Saturna, Patos, and Sucia. We turned toward them, climbing as we went. We leveled off at 3,000 feet as the lowest mists slid by overhead. Pender Island came into sight from Saturna, and Moresby from Pender. Our main worry was that the weather would close in ahead and behind at once.

The Saanich Peninsula emerged from the mists, and quite soon afterward we settled gently onto the wet asphalt. What had promised to be a fine spring day had turned into a foul afternoon. With IFR capability we could have followed our original plan without difficulty. Restricted to VFR it was difficult to do anything at all. It was not surprising that whenever John Milligan, Harvey's instructor, saw the two of us out at the Flying Club, he would ask: "Where are you guys not going today?"

Yet the clouds are themselves beautiful. One Saturday the sky was all but covered with a layer of broken cumulus at 2,500 feet, and dotted with convective rainstorms. One gray monster shrouded the peaks of Saltspring Island; another lay over Pender Island. I climbed to 2,000 feet and looked toward it.

It was beautiful. Yet it was more than beautiful; it was perfect. It must have been two or three miles across. It was awesome, like a mountain, an iceberg in the sky. Part bulbous, part fibrous, it rose perhaps to 10,000 feet, its crest an upburst of snow-white fluff. An opaque veil of rain, battleship-gray and striated, hung beneath it, apparently motionless, yet changing subtly from minute to minute. A white streamer of hail swathed its flank. Though massive, it was also weightless. Though weightless, it contained colossal power, fueled by the latent heat of condensing water vapor. Though powerful, faintly malevolent, and armed with fierce turbulence, it had no life. It was an inanimate expression of physical laws, as was my aircraft. Its Creator had wound it up and let it loose to play in the sky. And it was so beautiful. It was perfect.

Yet why did I have to fly to admire it so? From a mere 2,000 feet above the ground, why was my perspective different from that of the inhabitants of Saltspring Island, who even now heard me droning overhead? Because they were not free. The people of Pender Island could not choose whether it dumped a million gallons of rain on them or whether it passed a mile to one side. They were not free to inspect it from any angle they chose, or indeed to look down at it. They could not see it as I saw it, nor could they fear it as I feared it. At close quarters it would be a blinding mass of rain and mist, of hail, downdrafts and roiling turbulence, a floating hazard, a reef in the ocean of the sky. I knew that it was these things and was content to admire it from afar.

With an instrument rating I would be free to tread the gray halls of the sky, yet I still had to accumulate flight time under VFR. In the cloudy skies of spring, I had to cover my frustration with patience.

—29

Aerobic Exercises

Once upon a time, at a Flying Club open day, I was standing beside the Cessna 150 Aerobat, IDS, which was on static display. My job was to answer questions, be nice to people, encourage them to learn to fly, and otherwise stand there with a vacant grin wrapped around my face.

"Good afternoon, sir, are you interested in learning to fly?"

"I fly for Air Canada."

"Good afternoon, sir, are you interested in learning to fly?"

"Wouldn't get me up in one of them things for a million bucks."

"Good afternoon, sir, are you interested in learning to fly?"

"Used to fly Lancasters during the War. Haven't flown much since."

A new tactic is required: "Good afternoon, sir, do you fly much?"

And so it went on. After an extended period of this, my ego had turned a mottled green and crept in through the drain hole in the fuselage to hide in the dark. My feet hurt; my throat felt as if I had been eating broken hacksaw blades. I revived a little when someone with a genuine interest came along. I remarked in passing that the aircraft was built for aerobatics but that very few people flew such maneuvers. My victim transfixed me with the simple question: "Why not?"

I opened my mouth to answer, but nothing came out. Why not? Well why actually not? I was forced into vague mutterings. People do not want to spend the extra money. They do not like being upside down. They do not like abnormal g loadings. They think people might laugh at them. They think aerobatics might be dangerous. They think it is too difficult. They just plain do not want to fly aerobatics.

Why, then, do I fly aerobatics? For curiosity, for the challenge, and, above all, for the joy. The accident statistics are littered with people who thought they would try a little bit of aerobatics (or a little bit of flying in cloud or at night). Untutored curiosity is a surefire killer; I am curious about aerobatics.

All aircraft can enter aerobatic maneuvers, but not all of them can emerge unscathed. The big 182, XMY, is not built for aerobatics. I have no wish to test that assertion. XMY is equipped to carry me through the wind and cloud and rain. One day, all in good time, I will fly XMY on instruments. But there is IDS sitting on the asphalt or alive under the control of my fingers and toes. IDS is built for aerobatics. Sooner or later I must fly IDS in aerobatic flight.

In the back of my logbook is a slip of paper that reads:

> This is to certify that
> Tom Morrison
> has graduated as a(n)
> Aerobatic Pilot
> from the Victoria Flying Club
> this 25 day of August 1985.
>   J. W. Kaiser VRA 167192

No one ever sees that document because it is my secret. Some people, as soon as they earn their private license, buy the biggest set of wings insignia they can find and sew them onto the chest of whatever garment they wear to go flying. Why they do this is a mystery, because it has no effect on the successful outcome of the flight. I wear no visible wings, but I have my secret wings. They are the wings of an aerobatic pilot. They do have an effect on the successful outcome of the flight, and a beneficial one at that.

Some pilots write of defying gravity. But where is this defiance, and why? Gravity is like the will of a dancing partner. Without a partner the dance is mere calisthenics. It is the partner who makes the dance. What is the point in rolling and looping a spacecraft up there in the void? It is merely a test that the controls work, a mere gyration.

My engine and wings pull up into a vertical climb and, briefly, because I choose to do so, I defy gravity. I cash in all my reserves of kinetic energy and engine power and spend them in a vertical climb directly against gravity. Yet gravity and the friction of the air combine against me as I know they will. Just before the instant of bankruptcy, which I foresee precisely, I stamp full rudder, punching my foot toward the unattainable sky, and the aircraft cartwheels slowly, so slowly that I doubt my judgment. I am weightless in the slowly revolving aircraft.

As the nose drops, I chop engine power and the aircraft falls, as an upthrown dart, into a vertical dive. Because of gravity it is falling, falling toward the bottom of the sky nearly a mile distant. But I am not afraid that gravity will smash me into the ground, because of the air hissing thickly over my wings. As long as my airplane remains structurally whole, I cannot fall. It will remain whole because I am gentle with my wings, because a wise and gentle pilot taught me to fly. I have flown a hammerhead. Without gravity there could be no hammerhead, no aerobatic flight. I fly the hammerhead with the knowledge that banishes fear because I am an aerobatic pilot.

The bellowing of my engine and the swooshing air and my rolling, looping, cartwheeling wings flashing in the sunlight may reach down through the quiet sky to show ground-bound man what his own kind can do. But chiefly there is joy in the tumbling sky and the softly whirling earth.

Jack Kaiser and I took off into the first fine weather of spring. Jack had me demonstrate some of the maneuvers that Doug MacColl had taught me, but did not at once demolish my enthusiasm by demanding quality performance of these before going on to other things. "Other things" included loops, rolls, and barrel rolls.

Jack rounded off the lesson with what he said was a spin, followed by a hammerhead and a half loop with a snap half roll off the top. I knew that earth and sky swapped places with startling rapidity but, beyond that, the sequence was a mystery. To my surprise I felt no fear, only an overpowering urge to laugh. With heavy control pressures and unaccustomed g loadings, the lesson was physically tiring, and afterward I felt thoroughly wrung out. There was much to look forward to, however, in this fascinating realm of flight.

Straight looping and straight rolling maneuvers were fine, but maneuvers such as cloverleaves and barrel rolls, which involved simultaneous rolling and looping, had me thoroughly confused. Aerobatics in a Cessna 150 were a gentle affair. Nothing happened particularly fast, and all the basic maneuvers could be flown within the modest g loadings between 0 and +3. Sitting in your chair, by the way, you are experiencing +1g. If you were strapped in and the chair were to be turned upside down, you would experience –1g. Weightless in a spacecraft, you would be in 0g. A normal Cessna 152 is built to take +4.4g to –1.76g; the Aerobat is built for +6 to –3g; a purpose-built aerobatic aircraft is designed to withstand +9 to –6g. The body resists positive g better than negative g. Beyond +4g, without special equipment, vision deteriorates and blacking out may occur. Most negative g loads are uncomfortable, especially beyond –1g, which causes bloodshot eyes and headaches.

After two or three lessons I was able to fly loops, rolls, barrel rolls, and cloverleaves without Jack talking me through them. We started to fly sequences, using the airspeed built up at the end of one maneuver to begin the next one. This is easier said than done because the novice needs to resume level flight to collect his wits. The yachtsmen down on Cowichan Bay must have looked up in surprise at the mad little airplane cavorting about overhead.

Each time we returned to the airport, Jack would set me a series of practical and oral tests to improve my overall performance: "Tell me, young man, does the ASI over-read or under-read in a sideslip to the left, and why?"

"India Delta Sierra," says the tower, "You're-cleared-to-a-left-base-on-zero-eight-number-three-to-land-number-two-on-zero-eight-traffic-is-a-Bandeirante-two-miles-on-final-watch-out-for-the-Dash-Seven-turning-final-on-thirteen."

"Come on, answer the question."

And maximum-performance sideslips and power-off spot landings. "Misjudged the wind, didn't you? *Why?*"

Jack believed in giving value for money, and it astonished me how he managed his fantastic output of energy throughout the often very long days. Jack had led Air Force formation aerobatic teams in T-33s and Sabres and thought the F-5 a "nice little airplane, especially below 20,000 feet," so teaching basic aerobatics in a Cessna 150 was not too exciting for him.

"Young man," he remarked as we disentangled ourselves from the aircraft, "I enjoy flying with you, but you do choose some crummy airplanes to fly in."

Jack cleared me to fly aerobatics alone. After Doug's tuition I had flown nominally aerobatic maneuvers, but the first true solo aerobatics involve inverted flight, however brief. The actuality of aerobatics is turning upside down. Not without trepidation, I took off and climbed to 3,500 feet over the Cowichan Valley. I craned my neck and flew several wingovers to look for other aircraft. Finally, there being no just cause or impediment, down with the nose, 2,500 rpm on the tach, and the airspeed builds up past 100 knots. The slipstream rustles; that broken piece of plastic on the strut fairing whistles. Instead of floating in the sky, the aircraft settles into hard, bunched flight. Sneak back on the throttle to avoid overspeeding the engine; there is 115 knots—how about 120 for good measure? Up with the nose and full throttle as it comes up through the horizon, and 2.5g pushes me firmly into the seat. There is nothing but sky, absolutely nothing. Earth has gone away and left me alone in space.

I dare not look to either side. I have only blind faith that the aircraft will continue to pitch up and over. I throw my head back to see, with wonderful relief, Earth rising in the two smoked perspex slots in the cabin roof. Now the nose is on the way down, inverted, and the green ground is falling through the windshield. Ease back on the power in an inverted steep dive, sitting lightly in the seat. Keep the nose coming on around, and there is the sky appearing once more where it used to be long ago, so long ago, before I flew my first loop.

I flew some more loops, then two in a row, then rolls and barrel rolls, and one more loop just to make sure, then back to the patch. After tying the airplane down, I floated on air across the asphalt wearing an ear-to-ear grin.

"How did it go?" asked the girl behind the desk. I grinned. Strangers were standing at the counter. I had never seen them before. I grinned all over them. I wandered away down the corridor, still grinning, and floated out into the sunlit air.

But it was not all easy. There were botched maneuvers which ended in wild, rolling inverted dives accelerating briskly through 135 knots. Even at 3,500 feet, the trees flung themselves at me. A hundred and thirty-five knots straight down gives a descent rate of 13,500 feet per minute. It is not a situation conducive to the leisurely contemplation of the view, spectacular through it may be.

Once I flew a practice and a lesson on the same day. The lesson included Cuban eights, which consist, in part, of rolling upright from an inverted steep dive. I overdosed on aerobatics that day, and my sleep was shot through with nightmares. I awoke in the dark to find the bed straight and level but, as soon as my eyelids fell shut, the inverted steep dives began again and the trees hurled themselves at me.

The weather turned foul once more, so I managed only three practices in as many months. The novice aerobatic pilot needs 4,000 feet of clear sky, for reasons which should be obvious, and this was simply not available when needed. Jack Kaiser was busy teaching new instructors. I gradually lost my skills without knowing how and without being able to do anything about it. In the end I gave up until more tuition was forthcoming.

Not until mid-July did Jack become free of his commitments. I explained my problems to him, which set the stage for a most brilliant piece of teaching.

Any aircraft has a natural maneuvering pace. The aerodynamic explanation is no doubt very complicated, involving moments of inertia and good stuff like that, but the empirical fact is not. Even something as basic as rolling into a gently banked turn can be done too slowly, in which case it is sloppy; too quickly, in which case it is rough; or at the aircraft's natural pace. The pilot who unconsciously recognizes the aircraft's natural pace flies smoothly; the one who does not flies roughly.

In normal, everyday flight this fact is of limited consequence. In aerobatic flight in a low-powered aircraft, it is everything. Indeed, without this feel, aerobatics cannot be flown successfully in such an aircraft. The aircraft cannot be dragged through by the scruff of its neck, nor can the maneuver be performed too slowly, as in either case the aircraft will run out of airspeed halfway through. A Cessna 150 has limited power in relation to its weight, and there are few options on how a maneuver can be flown. Jack achieved a harmony between the pace of his teaching and the natural pace of the aircraft. All of a sudden I was flying aerobatics instead of merely going through the motions.

After a couple of deeply satisfying practices and a lesson: "Come on, let's wrap this thing up." This was to be an aerobatic flight test. Jack briefed me before we took off: "I want you to show me this sequence: first a loop, then a barrel roll left, a cloverleaf right, a cloverleaf left, a stall turn (that thing you call a hammerhead), an aileron roll right, then a half roll left—enter it at 110 knots—half loop out coming up to 135 knots, then up into another half loop with a righthand half roll off the top." I stared at him in amazement.

We lined up behind another aircraft to take off. "Look at him drift," said Jack as the other airplane, oblivious of this criticism, drifted away in a slight crosswind. The test would be on as soon as I opened the throttle.

We flew some warming-up exercises over Cowichan Bay. The yachts looked up at us; we looked up at them. A ballpoint pen emerged from a hiding place and floated hesitantly in the middle of the cabin. Jack grabbed it as it wandered past his face.

For the prescribed sequence I insisted on climbing to 4,000 feet as I would surely lose a great amount of height in the forthcoming evolutions. After going through the sequence, I was surprised to emerge in level flight at 3,000 feet. I drew breath.

"Show me a forty-five-degree barrel roll around Shawnigan Lake," said Jack, pointing to the burnished lake gleaming between the hills. I did so.

"Show me a three-quarter-turn spin to the right and come out facing Mount Baker. Don't think about it. Do it. Now." I presented him with the required view of Mount Baker dead center in the windshield.

"Let's go home." And that was that.

The "basic" aerobatics course is exactly that. It teaches the pilot to fly the basic maneuvers safely and for his own enjoyment. They are the loop, aileron roll, barrel roll, cloverleaf, Cuban eight, stall turn or hammerhead, snap roll, Immelmann, and precision spin. Some people will say that a Cessna 150 will not fly aerobatics, to which others would reply that it can fly some uncommonly good imitations, and it will be a long time before the novice exhausts its possibilities.

There is a distinction between basic and advanced aerobatics. Basic aerobatics will satisfy most of us and make us better pilots. They can be flown in the aerobatic versions of common aircraft such as the Cessna 150, Beech Musketeer, and Citabria. The aerobatic models have stronger structures to withstand the heavier loads placed on the airframe. They are not designed for negative-g maneuvers or sustained inverted flight, because the engine is designed to function right side up and dislikes being turned upside down (or subjected to negative, hanging-in-the-straps, g, which amounts to the same thing). The brief periods of inverted flight in the basic maneuvers are, or should be, carried out in slightly positive g.

Advanced aerobatics are without limit. An aerobatics dictionary lists 100,000 different maneuvers. Advanced aerobatics involve sustained inverted flight and severe negative as well as positive g. These can be flown only in purpose-built aerobatic aircraft such as the Zlin, Pitts Special, Kristen Eagle, and others. To attempt them in basic aerobatic aircraft can be as dangerous as attempting basic aerobatics in aircraft not built for aerobatics at all.

Formation aerobatics are another, more advanced, form of the art. The airshow exhibitions of low-level and formation aerobatics can be flown safely only by highly experienced professional pilots, and then only with ceaseless practice. Very few nonprofessional pilots can afford the time or money necessary for enough practice to fly them safely. All this does not alter the fact that the low-time, nonprofessional pilot can still derive immense benefit and pleasure from the surprisingly gentle art of aerobatic flight.

—30———————————

Cloud Nine

The summer of 1985 came late to Vancouver Island. Even in early June the weather was still uncertain and changeable. Toward the middle of the month, the sky finally dried out, and barely a drop of rain fell until September. Huge forest fires raged in the interior of British Columbia. On the island the fire hazard went from "high" to "extreme" to "critical," until the forestry people ran out of words to describe it. The forests were closed to public access for a record 67 days. Day after day the sun shone from calm, cloudless skies. VFR pilots scarcely needed to check the weather. IFR pilots forgot how to fly instruments. "Clear all over" was the weatherman's reply to all inquiries.

Only gradually did the long hot summer give way to the coolness and damp of autumn. The ground was so parched after the drought that it took two weeks of continuous rain before the creeks ran once more in the forests. For the pilots it had been a summer to remember. My friends and I had flown far and wide over British Columbia and across the border into Washington state. I had made good use of the cloudless weather and had built up the hours of VFR cross-country flying that were mandatory to gain an instrument rating.

Nevertheless, the road to the instrument rating stretched ahead ever more daunting, ever more wearing to the patience. Whereas in the course of time so many VFR flights had been weathered out, now it was impossible to find instrument conditions in which to learn IFR. Our flight through the clouds down Washington way in the spring of 1984 had convinced me that IFR was, in actuality, a safe, simple, and convenient method of cruising the skies, apart from its aesthetic qualities. This certain knowledge sustained me through the baffling complexities of learning how to do it. Even so, I spent the next two years learning to fly on instruments without ever entering cloud.

The clear days of an extraordinarily cold autumn followed each other in endless succession. The fifty hours of VFR cross-country flight seems to be of doubtful relevance. Yet there is no requirement that the candidate for the instrument rating shall spend any time flying in real instrument conditions. It is possible, actually not uncommon, for a pilot to obtain his instrument rating without ever having flown in cloud.

I had not flown on instruments for five and a half months. Some people lose their skills in that time through lack of practice, but I found that the material had settled in my mind. Within fifty miles of Victoria are four Canadian airports with instrument approaches, besides Victoria itself. Within a two-hour flight it was possible to fly a triangular route, involving four instrument approaches, complete with navigation from one airport to another and all the interactions with air traffic control.

For the trainee it was more grueling than any actual IFR flight. Immediately after takeoff, on went the hood. No sooner was the aircraft established in cruising flight than it was time to get the ATIS for the destination, get out the approach plate, tune the radios, and fly the airplane all at the same time. In clear weather the radio carried a continuous babble between air traffic control and both IFR and VFR traffic. Every man and his dog could see what was going on except me. At times I had to listen on two radios—one on the ATIS frequency, one on the ATC frequency—and then Jack would chip in exactly as the controller shot a clearance to me. In between times I had to tune and listen for the Morse identifiers of the navaids I was trying to use. The voices in my headphones became a wall of noise, and all I could do was wait for someone to give up.

"Aviate, navigate, communicate" is an old pilots' saying, and never is it more true than when flying single-pilot IFR. The pilot must, above all, keep the aircraft under control and pointed in the right direction. Next he must be sure of his position. Third (and however insistent the voices on the radio may be, it must remain third), he must communicate with ATC in its own language. After all, it is physically possible to complete an IFR flight without talking to anyone at all. It is just that people disapprove of it, it is illegal, inconvenient to other users of the system, and related considerations.

"X-Ray Mike Yankee you're cleared to the Vancouver airport straight-in ILS zero eight approach steer zero five zero vectors to intercept descend to and maintain two thousand until established on the localizer report the tower eighteen seven Ross inbound" does not mean a vast amount to any normal user of the English language. It is a language, very terse, each word having a precisely defined meaning, which the trainee must learn.

At the same time, Jack's demands for precision became more and more stringent. In a brief moment of undisturbed cruising flight, he remarked: "You are thirty feet too high." We were flying at 3,000 feet. An error of 30 feet represented just 1%. Because the instrument providing this information had its own small errors and because we were flying over rocky islands covered with tall trees and surrounded by a sea that rose and fell with the tide, the instrument's statement that we were flying at 3,030 feet merely begged the question, "Above what?" The next question was, "So what?" Nevertheless, the IFR clearance was to fly at 3,000 feet as indicated by the altimeter, and not 3,030 feet. The bald statement, "You are thirty feet too high," was the absolute and precise truth.

Each approach would be flown to the decision height on an ILS approach or the minimum descent altitude on a non-precision approach. At the appropriate moment Jack would say, "Look up!" There would be a black runway surrounded by green grass, sometimes splashed with snow, because it was a cold autumn. Or a circling approach might have to be flown at the precise altitude stated on the approach plate by reference both to the instruments and to the outside world as seen by peering out from under the hood. We would either make a touch-and-go landing or go at once into the missed approach procedure. Because there was no time in the two hours to stop and collect my wits, it was by no means easy.

I seethed with indignation at the vagaries of the weather. By the end of 1985, we had flown seven exercises on IFR flight plans, all of them in the winter months, all of them on pre-arranged dates. Statistically the probability of making a VFR cross-country flight with those preconditions was down around 10%. For all seven IFR exercises the sky was not merely good VMC, it was cloudless. Just once I felt the aircraft being hit by someone with very large, soft boxing gloves and looked out to see the mother-of-pearl interior of a minute cumulus cloud.

The low-lying stratus and stratocumulus decks that made IFR so desirable on the Pacific coast were just not there. I knew that cloud ceilings did not always hang exactly on the approach plate minima. I knew that the runway did not appear as if by magic at exactly one mile or some other specified distance. I was learning to herd the aircraft around the sky according to exact numbers, but I was not learning to fly IFR. It was too much "let's pretend." Nevertheless, I gradually gained control over the whole operation beyond the minute-to-minute progress of the flight.

Even so, the task of getting it all together IFR-wise remained formidable. Jeremy Rimmer, Tom Spreen, and I sat around hangar-flying in Molly's Coffee Shop one morning. I asked Jeremy: "Did you ever count how many knobs and switches XMY has in the avionics stack? Not even the total—just the ones the pilot has to fiddle with all the time under IFR?" Jeremy looked out of the window at the Flying Firemen's elderly Canso and pondered for a while.

"Eight or nine?"

"Jeremy," I replied, "there are forty-three."

After a mild January, February 1986 came and dumped another foot of snow on us to make one of the most severe winters in forty years. Jack had been busy all January with several people who had to get their instrument ratings in a hurry, but with a vicious, occluded front producing freezing rain and wet snow all over southwestern British Columbia, he telephoned me: "You want to fly weather? Come on out and let's fly some weather." That Saturday the risk of airframe ice was so severe that no one was flying at all, so we flew the simulator instead. The following day matters had improved somewhat, and we launched for Abbotsford and Vancouver.

We flew into cloud at 2,500 feet on the way out to the Victoria beacon. The cloud was thin and patchy, giving views of brown islands seamed with snow before the mists slid by beneath and around us again. Inbound from White Rock things became more serious. The airfield was in the middle of a snowstorm; the tower controller reported that visibility was less than a mile and that he had the runway lights full bright for us. Riding the crossed beams of the ILS, I could hear snow rustling against the aircraft's skin. Exactly on decision height, I looked up to see the approach lights, but otherwise everything was solid white. We climbed away for an NDB approach.

"Conditions are below NDB minima, aren't they?" I asked. Jack nodded. We went on with the approach. In the procedure turn we came out into a gray-white world of snow-covered fields and a silk-white sky. It was an unnecessary mental effort even to try to estimate my position in terms of visual landmarks. The landscape was interesting, but it was meaningless. XMY was a creature of the fogs and clouds. We plunged back into the rustling snow.

My world was laid out in mauve print on the approach plate clipped to the yoke. My position in that world was displayed by the instruments, each of whose wavering needles pleaded for its share of my attention. Suddenly one would scream at me: "I am All Wrong and getting worse. I have been wandering and you wouldn't come and get me." I would nudge the aircraft with hand and foot to soothe its silent cries. Or I might watch the needle's slow drift and so sense the unfelt wind wafting me off the appointed track. Another gentle nudge would slew the aircraft crabwise along the guiding beam.

On reaching the missed approach point, 600 feet above the ground, we could see nothing, not even the runway lights. The people on the ground heard our snarling propeller as we pulled up into the cloud; perhaps they saw a shadow fleetingly through the falling snow. I saw something black under my left elbow, which was evidently the runway, but it was of no further interest.

At 4,000 feet a splatter of ice built up on the windshield, and I looked out to see rime ice on the leading edges of the wings and struts. We soon emerged into clear air near Vancouver. The controller pointed out that we had a Boeing 727 breathing down our necks and urged us to maintain speed. "Maintaining speed," according to Jack, meant cruising power and 3° of nose-down pitch, which had us moving along at 150 knots.

The next problem was how to get the aircraft slowed down to make a landing, at which I failed entirely. The wild bouncing and sliding impacts with the runway were the worst landing I had made since before going solo. The weather having partially cleared, on went the hated hood for the flight back to Victoria. The consolation was that flying by instruments in reality was so easy. The cloud was real. If it was there, it was there: if it was not there, it was not there.

A week later we took off into a rainy sky, bound for Vancouver. Harvey Taggart had come along for the ride. The cloud base was at 1,500 feet, but at 3,000 feet we were above the lowest cloud deck. We had not been airborne for long when Jack turned to me and said, "Young man, you are ready for your flight test." Just what had made him so sure so suddenly was beyond me. A quilted deck of cloud unrolled beneath us. Rain fell from a high overcast in a sky the color of watered milk. Five miles away a Boeing 767 floated in the void. It was a dull Sunday afternoon, and few people were about.

The approach controller vectored us toward the ILS, and we sank down toward the cloud. Visibility faded, and I paid progressively more attention to the instruments. Soon I noticed out of the corner of my eye that we were, indeed, in cloud. The DME clocked off the miles as we sped on down the ILS beams. At one moment we were in cloud; a split second later my peripheral vision took in an impression of solid objects, runway lights, and a glaucous, wind-roughened sea.

We did not land because of other aircraft behind us having prior claims, but instead enfolded ourselves once more in the cloud from which we had so briefly emerged. After ten minutes or so we were on course for Victoria in that other world of the clouds. It was a very real world, with a floor and a ceiling, and lateral dimensions rendered indefinite by distance, yet in it there was no solid object other than ourselves. It was not two-dimensional like the sea, and therefore understandably trackless.

It seemed that this swelling ridge, this valley, should in some way be features with a degree of permanence by which I could find my way yesterday, today, and tomorrow. But they were not. They would change their topography by the hour, if not by the minute, nor would they ever sustain any fixed relationship with the downstairs world from which we had temporarily escaped. This cloud world, unlike the solid and liquid worlds, supported no life. No creatures browsed its acres or hunted each other among its caves and canyons. Nor could man shape it in any way, or leave any trace of his existence on it.

Soon it became necessary to study the detailed instructions laid out in front of me on how to return to the solid world below. The plate stated that if I were to fly through this cloud world along an invisible concept called the Vancouver 215° radial until I was 32 electronically indicated miles from the source of that radial, and if I then were to turn left to steer 130° according to a little piece of metal that I kept shut up in a box, I would come to a magic beam. If I were then to turn further left to follow that beam and sink down through the cloud according to its instructions, I would thereby come back to the world of solid objects at a locality where my aircraft would find it convenient, and in the end necessary, to rest.

We flew into hanging veils of rain and mist, and the cloud world faded from our sight as though our transition from one world to another should be accomplished secretly. In due course we found the magic beam we were looking for. To follow the beam so as to avoid the large masses of extremely solid rock not far beneath us required a degree of concentration that made further meditation inappropriate.

At 4,000 feet we had been butting directly into a 40-knot wind from the west. Winds on the ground were light and easterly. A bout of fierce turbulence announced our passage from the upper air, which was shearing and tearing over the air near the ground. A gap in the cloud revealed the Mill Bay shoreline and, as I looked out at the wet mist which was again flowing around the wing, I reflected for a split second on the length and strangeness of the road I had traveled since my first tremulous flights through this same piece of sky three years before. We broke out into clear air over the Saanich Inlet in time to slow down the aircraft for a long, floating landing on a runway gleaming in the rain.

"Well," asked Jack as we taxied in, "Are you happy with that flight?"

"Yes," I replied with emphasis.

"OK, we'll fix a date for your flight test."

—31

The Last Battle

Private and commercial flight tests were administered at Victoria on any day mutually convenient to examiner and examinee. The examiner had a full-time job as a pilot and was a government-appointed examiner in his spare time. The test was absolutely fair, with no tricks. If the examiner was John Addison, who had a profound love of flight and airplanes, the test could be a lot of fun.

The IFR flight test was a different story. It was administered on weekdays only by a small army of full-time inspectors who apparently did nothing else. Every instrument pilot must have an annual "check ride," so they kept fairly busy.

Testing was done at Vancouver airport. The candidate had, therefore, to make an appointment, absent himself from work for a day, fly to Vancouver, take the test, and fly back again. For the initial test the weather had to be VFR so that the as-yet VFR-restricted pilot could fly there. The test had to be carried out in VFR conditions. If the candidate failed, he would have to fly home under VFR. Even if he passed, he might be too exhausted to fly home IFR. The chances of obtaining VFR weather on a predetermined day in winter were, to say the least, uncertain.

The inspectors were reputed to be ogres. The line between a pass and a fail was very fine. Disturbing reports came back of tests failed for reasons that were a mystery to all concerned. Competent pilots became blithering idiots. Some of the reasons were more obvious. One poor kid had made an appointment with the chief ogre for 1:00 P.M. on a certain day. Presenting himself at the specified time and place, he was told that the inspector was in a meeting. Two hours later the man emerged from the meeting in a foul mood. By this time the candidate was hungry, tired,

179

and in a pitiable state of nerves, which was by no means palliated when the inspector began hazing him on the alleged grounds that his papers were not in order. Needless to say, he failed the test that followed. Such prospects did nothing for my morale.

When the appointed day arrived, I was in an advanced state of nerves. It was March 13th, an omen which I sought to disregard. I had not left a large amount of spare time. The aircraft, XMY, which was supposed to have been fueled, had nearly empty tanks, causing further delay. One of the navigation radios had a minor glitch which I had not seen before; I did not even know if it was significant or not. I blasted off from Victoria anyway, under a gray overcast. Near Vancouver I was involved in a minor altercation with one of the controllers. I pulled off such a horrendously bad landing that I wondered if I had damaged the nosewheel. Things were not shaping up well. I parked the aircraft and went into the flight test office.

The inspector turned out to be an amiable character named Don Davidson. Don had me explain the weather situation to him in detail and then examined me rigorously on IFR procedures, weather minima, and the like. Then we went flying.

I put on the hood before we took off, peering out from under it. As we climbed through 200 feet, I said, "I'm going on instruments, *now*." At that point it dawned on me that I was not entirely sure what I was supposed to be doing, and this vague uncertainty remained for the rest of the flight. After Jack Kaiser's streams of conversation, philosophy, and comment, punctuated with occasional objurgations, the utter silence from the right seat was unnerving. I was required to use a radio callsign other than the aircraft's registration letters, in this case "Regs Five Bravo." I disliked it. The callsign had the function of identifying the aircraft to the air traffic controllers as being on an IFR flight test, the significance of which was to appear by and by.

If you watch the exhaust of a turbine-powered aircraft in flight, you will see occasional puffs of thin black smoke. I had the sensation that small mistakes were appearing, whipping away in the slipstream like those puffs of black smoke. Unfortunately, they were to thicken during the test to a solid black trail.

I was alarmed to see that I had missed the White Rock beacon by a substantial margin without knowing why. We started an NDB approach into Abbotsford. Part of the procedure consisted of leveling off at 1,400 feet. Just above 1,400 feet there was some insignificant distraction, and the next time I looked at the altimeter, we were down to 1,200 feet, a very serious error. I climbed back to 1,400 feet as quickly as possible, but the damage had been done. I was on final approach with flaps fully extended when Don said, "You just flew into a fog bank." I poured on the power and climbed away in the missed approach.

Don told me to obtain a clearance to hold at either the White Rock beacon or the Vancouver VOR. Because White Rock had a published holding procedure, I asked the controller for a hold there. A holding pattern is a racetrack-shaped circuit used under IFR to keep an aircraft circling near a "holding fix" to allow for traffic spacing. Its apparent simplicity, like many things in aviation, is deceptive. If the long axis of the holding pattern is across the wind, it is more difficult to keep the circuit in shape. I was surprised when the controller cleared me to fly a holding pattern that was askew to the one published on the IFR charts and more difficult to follow, with no apparent reason for the change.

For several days I wondered why the controller had chosen this particular alignment for the hold. I then realized that the long axis of this hold was exactly across the 3,000-foot wind published for that time by the aviation weather office.* It took a few more days of deduction and inquiry to discover that there was connivance between some inspectors and the air traffic controllers to make life difficult for flight test candidates. The use of a special radio callsign made it easy to do this. I could not help thinking that if an inspector had to enlist the controllers' help to discover whether a pilot was competent to fly IFR, perhaps he was in the wrong profession.

The ground track of my attempt at a holding pattern would have resembled a cat's cradle. There was an audible sigh from the right seat as I charged around the (supposed) racetrack pattern again and again. A little gremlin whispered in my ear: "Hang tough! Don't give up! You can still pull this mess out of the fire." Nevertheless, I wondered who would give up first, me or my passenger. "Get a clearance back to Vancouver," he said wearily. The controller tried to send me back to Abbotsford, but I explained that we had seen enough of the place for now. At least Don had not told me there and then that I had failed. I put this small nightmare behind me and set affairs in order for the approach to Vancouver.

As mentioned previously, the localizer and glideslope beams of an instrument landing system become narrower toward the transmitters so

---

* Aviation weather offices forecast the speed and direction of winds aloft for a series of altitudes, of which 3,000 feet is one.

that over the runway threshold they are very narrow indeed. Therefore, the closer the aircraft is to the runway, the more skittish the ILS needles in the cockpit become. Close in, within five miles, changing the aircraft's attitude by one or two degrees suffices to sneak the needles back into their required positions. If the novice instrument pilot does not have them well centered at this stage, the pressure is on to get back on track quickly. He makes a correction of perhaps 10°. To his alarm, the needle swings out to full-scale deflection on the opposite side of the dial before he can turn the aircraft in time to catch it, resulting in an even wilder attempt to turn back the other way. If he does not make the attempt, he will stay off the beam. If he does make the attempt, the chances are that he will fly right across it again. All the time the aircraft is flying toward the runway at a mile every forty-five seconds, and the beam is becoming narrower and narrower. It is (and was) a hopeless situation.

"You are visual," Don announced, and we landed. "Come into the office," he said as we deplaned. "You don't need any paperwork." At that point I knew I had failed the test. Had I passed, I would have needed my license for his endorsement. No paperwork, no endorsement, failed test.

My fears were confirmed by direct inquiry. Don was highly complimentary about the things I had done well and said he had enjoyed flying with me. He explained in detail what had gone wrong and why. It was the cheapest flying lesson I ever had. My instinct to keep fighting every inch of the way had been correct. I had failed the test only in the last minute or two before landing. I booked another test for March 26.

I returned to my faithful aircraft and wrapped it around me, shutting myself into its warm interior, bruised, hurt, and utterly exhausted. This was the first major test which I had failed in fifteen years. I let XMY's soothing wings waft me back to the slate-gray islands on the tarnished silver sea. As Victoria airport came into sight, the unpleasant fact came to mind that I was going to have to explain myself to the people at the Flying Club. The prospect was unappealing. By the time I taxied in, I was prepared to put a bold face on it: There were no real consequences attached; it had been good experience; it had uncovered some flaws that needed uncovering; there was nothing for it but to try again.

March 26 got off to a bad start. I awoke at five o'clock in the morning. My job was going badly, flying was going badly, so the black thoughts which settle on the mind at such an hour were plentiful. If it was not the thirteenth of the month, it was a multiple of it. The weather forecast was for marginal VFR in the morning, becoming IFR in the afternoon, so I thankfully canceled the test.

I flew three more lessons with Jack Kaiser. The first one was in cloud and rain all the way. Jack was fulsome in his praise. The second exercise was under the hood in a cloudless sky. Had it been a test, I would have failed. The third was a short one; my crime sheet was clean. The test now rose up before me as an impassable barrier. There would always be the hidden snag, some small and apparently inconsequential rule that I would break. I knew that I could fly actual IFR with the greatest of ease, but for passing the test my self-confidence was in small pieces with torn edges, stuffed into a brown Transport Canada envelope.

The private pilot, the night pilot, and the aerobatic pilot all start with some basic instruction. There comes a point when the instructor knows that the pupil must fly by himself; otherwise he cannot grow as a pilot. Training for the instrument rating is longer and harder than that for the private license, yet the pupil cannot fly by himself in instrument conditions until he has passed the test. It is as if a new private pilot were not allowed to fly solo until after the private pilot flight test. The instrument candidate cannot even file an IFR flight plan in perfect weather. One of the absurdities of the system is that at no time is the candidate ever required to fly in cloud. No one even cares. Stories abound of pilots who went through the training and passed the flight test without ever flying in cloud. They then either never dared to do so or scared themselves badly when they did so for the first time alone.

April 3 dawned calm beneath a high overcast. I slept well and breakfasted on a goose egg fried with bacon. A friend had given me the huge egg, and I was on hissing terms with the goose that had laid it. Geese are more intelligent than some humans, and I hoped that a modicum of goose sense would go with me. I allowed ample time, prepared at leisure, and took off promptly. On the radio I heard an altercation between a controller and "Regs One Alpha." I thought of some unfortunate pilot sweating under a hood, busy failing his flight test. Why couldn't the Wright brothers have stuck to bicycles?

I landed, taxied up to the parking spot allocated to IFR flight tests, and poured a cup of tea from my thermos. A yellow and black square-tailed Cessna 310 taxied up beside me, evidently the ill-starred Regs One Alpha. The pilot and an ogre deplaned. The ogre looked at me, looked at his watch, and scowled. I directed an unspoken malediction at him. It was only midday, and I was not due to be there until one o'clock. Still, I did not have to worry about him for another three quarters of an hour.

At 12:45 P.M. promptly I went into the inspectors' office. There were two ogres inside, to whom I announced my name and intentions. They looked at me like something the cat had brought in and responded: "There's been a change of plan. Mike Bradley's on his way out here to fly the test."

I had spoken to Mike Bradley by telephone before and had heard a warm-hearted, no-nonsense voice on the other end of the line. He had been an Air Force pilot with Jack Kaiser, and I knew the test would be straightforward, with no fancy trickery. He was a short, stocky man whose craggy features were ever ready to break into a smile that had, perforce, to be suppressed by the demands of his job. After a series of searching questions, we went out to the aircraft.

The flight test was uneventful. There were no tricks. Things went wrong, but I extricated myself from them. I broke rules, but none that imperiled the flight. On the way back to Vancouver, I looked up to find that we were in cloud. Snow streamed by beneath us; the aircraft bucked and rolled.

This time two gremlins perched on my shoulders. The bad gremlin had been there all the time. It hissed: "You've failed the test. You screwed up and *he noticed*. You're way outside specified tolerances for heading, altitude, and track. Tell him you can't hack it. Go on, give up and go home. You can't unscramble eggs." The good gremlin said: "That's nonsense. You're flying IFR, not cooking, and you can unscramble things, if not eggs. He can't see inside your brain. The game's not over until it's finished. You can win on what you're going to do, not on what you've done. Besides, you're in cloud. You like flying in cloud. The stupidest place in the world to decide that you can't hack it is inside a cloud." So we came to Vancouver, flew down the ILS beams, and landed without a word passing between us.

Mike was already walking away from the aircraft when I could stand it no longer. "Do I bring any paperwork with me?" In this crazy world of make-believe, where people bored holes in clear skies with hoods over their eyes and where "Regulations Six Alpha" was an aircraft callsign, everything was oblique, a sidestep from reality. If you did not think obliquely, if you did not sidestep correctly, you failed the test. Thus my inquiry was also oblique.

"Just your license," was the reply. I had passed the test. When I confirmed this by direct inquiry, Mike looked at me as if to say: "Of course you did. Isn't it obvious?" His verdict was: "There were some violations on which I could have failed you, but I think you have potential, so I'm going to give you a Class Two. Congratulations."

XMY wafted me back to Victoria, although I was so happy that I could have flown back without the aid of that curious invention, the flying machine. A heart-warming welcome awaited me at the Flying Club. I telephoned Jack Kaiser to give him the good news and to thank him for his patient instruction. He replied: "You're welcome. It's been a lot of fun."

And it had.

32

Cleared for the Approach

"X-Ray Mike Yankee you're cleared to the Victoria airport straight-in ILS zero eight approach steer one one zero for vectors to intercept the localizer."

I am in thick cloud, although a small gap showed me the brown earth behind a veil of racing snow. I hear the snow rustling against the aircraft's hide. Precipitation static popples in my headphones. At 4,000 feet the outside air thermometer shows a temperature a few degrees above freezing. I keep an anxious eye on the beads of moisture running back across the wing strut. As long as they keep running and do not turn to ice, all is well. In a real pinch I can tell the gentleman behind his radar screen that I need to get down quicker and see what happens. It is only the Cowichan Valley below me anyway.

Today I have flown my first solo flight in instrument conditions. If a road is defined by its mileposts, learning to fly is defined by first solos. The first solo flight of all, when the fledgling enters free flight alone, has the firmest hold on the imagination of those who have not flown and the recollections of those who have. Yet the first solo flight is but the first of such excursions. Next comes the first solo cross-country flight, and perhaps the first night solo and the first solo aerobatic flight, but looming up greater than these is the first solo flight through the clouds.

As the mariner sees the mountain wave rearing out of a storm-lashed sea, so too must the new instrument pilot regard this flight as the testing of himself and his craft. Unlike the mariner, the new instrument pilot can duck the punch. On days of low cloud, wind, and rain, he can pretend that he had no plans to fly. He can file and fly an IFR flight plan when there are but a few clouds about. He can go on flying approaches under the hood with a friend riding as safety pilot forever and a day. And he will be fooling himself. In the end, deliberately and alone, he must immerse himself in the gray-white interior of the cloud.

He will look outside and see no clue of any kind as to the aircraft's attitude, altitude, heading, or position, or even of its passage through the air. He will look at the instruments in front of him and will know all of these things. He levels off from a climb; his mind tells him that he is diving back toward the earth. He looks at the instruments and knows that this is not so. In straight and level flight a gremlin tells him that he is in a turn or, more insidiously, that he should be turning and should really be heading over *that* way. He looks at the instruments and tells the gremlin to shut up and that its services are not required at this time.

His mind tells him that the engine is running roughly. He scans the oil temperature and pressure gauges, the tachometer, the exhaust gas temperature gauge, the cylinder head temperature gauge, and the fuel gauges, and knows that all is well. Whatever other illusions his mind devises, even if it tells him that the aircraft is doing snap rolls, he looks at the instruments and sees that all is well. Thus he continues his cruising flight through the clouds with a quiet smile.

We have been turning on radar vectors, and here is the localizer needle creeping in toward the center of the dial. The glideslope needle is alive, if not fully awake. We turn onto the localizer. Here comes the glideslope. Start down. Mixture rich, prop fine pitch, carb heat hot, throttle back to fourteen inches of manifold pressure, flaps 10°.

"X-Ray Mike Yankee you're nine miles on final radar service terminated contact Victoria tower now on nineteen point seven."

"X-Ray Mike Yankee Victoria tower nineteen seven thanks good day."

"S'long."

Click over to the other radio.

"Victoria tower X-Ray Mike Yankee eight on final with Kilo."

"X-Ray Mike Yankee roger report Mill Bay inbound."

"Mike Yankee."

We're still in the clag. Now get back on the localizer and add a bit more power to stay on the glideslope. It's amazing how easily the thing seems to hang in there sometimes. At what height are we supposed to cross Mill Bay? 1,390 feet. How's the altitude doing? 2,700 feet, so we are OK for a bit. Hey, don't tell anybody, but this is a leadpipe cinch. When you've got a real horizon outside, you use it. When it's all white outside, you use this gizmo inside the airplane. Yes, but this isn't "hard

IFR" with ice and thunderstorms like they're always writing about in *Flying* magazine. You bet it isn't. That's what I've got a brain for, to stay out of that kind of stuff.

Here we are all of a sudden out in the clear. It is raining. Is that a runway I see before me? Probably. Just hang in there with the magic for a little while. Give them a landing light. Now look again. Yes, that is the airport and we are not even over Mill Bay. Just keep on trucking. Give him a yell over the Mill Bay beacon.

"X-Ray Mike Yankee Mill Bay inbound."

"X-Ray Mike Yankee number two traffic on left base."

"Mike Yankee looking."

There's the other guy turning onto final approach. Two things that ought to be cold and wet—a runway and a dog's nose. Cold, wet runways are nice to land on.

The other fellow has landed. Oh, he's taking off again. Power back to twelve inches of manifold pressure, let the airspeed come back to 80 knots, flaps 20°. Check the windsock, about 5 knots and not enough crosswind to worry about. Flaps 40°. Check the airspeed—feels good, sounds good, 67 knots, that's about right so leave it alone.

"X-Ray Mike Yankee cleared to land."

"Mike Yankee."

Now begin to flare out over the runway and hold the nose up, power to idle just off the ground, and hold the nose up still more firmly now. A yowling of air tearing away from the flaps, beep from the stall warning, and the main wheels brush the wet asphalt. Now let the nosewheel down just as it flops of its own accord, and we are down, slowing, and turning off the runway.

And do you know? It was so easy. It was a piece of cake.